√ 3

ADVENTURE IN COURAGE

The Story of Theodore Roosevelt

ADVENTURE
IN COURAGE

The Story of Theodore Roosevelt

by FRANCES CAVANAH
ILLUSTRATED BY GRACE PAULL

RAND McNALLY & COMPANY
Chicago · New York · San Francisco

This book is dedicated to
my brother

NEALE CAVANAH

"I PUT MYSELF in the way of things happening,
and they happened," Theodore Roosevelt once said.
His sixty years were a series
of adventures—more adventures than
could possibly be crowded into a single volume.
This book tells a part of his story—his early adventure in courage.
It begins in 1866 when he was eight
years old, and it takes him up to the beginning
of a new century when he became President
of the United States. The same high courage
that was his distinguishing trait in later years
was the magic touchstone that enabled him to change from
a shy, sickly child into one of the most vigorous
and colorful leaders of his time.

F. C.

ACKNOWLEDGMENTS

IN WRITING this story, the author combed old newspaper files to find contemporary accounts that showed Theodore Roosevelt as the people of his own time saw him. Letters and books by relatives and friends have shown him as he appeared to those who knew him most intimately, and his *Autobiography* was an important source of information. Theodore Roosevelt's early letters and *Diaries,* which he began as a young boy nicknamed Teedie, gave fascinating glimpses of life with his parents; with his older sister Anna or Bamie (later Mrs. William S. Cowles); with a younger sister Corinne or Conie (later Mrs. Douglas Robinson); and with his younger brother Elliott, or Ellie (later to become the father of Eleanor Roosevelt). Theodore Roosevelt's letters as a man provided an equally warm and intimate picture of his life with his wife Edith and their children. The *Annual Reports* of the New York Children's Aid Society helped to round out the picture of the President's father, the first Theodore Roosevelt.

There is not space to give the long list of sources consulted, but especially helpful were the books by Hermann Hagedorn, well-known authority on his subject, and a founder and former director of the Theodore Roosevelt Association; and *Theodore Roosevelt, the Formative Years,* the first volume of a new definitive biography by Carlton Putnam. The author wishes to thank Leslie C. Stratton, present director of the Theodore Roosevelt Association for his help, encouragement, and many courtesies, and Mr. Stratton as well as Mrs. Harold Kraft, curator at Sagamore Hill, for the interesting and profitable hours spent in two of the homes, now museums, in which Theodore Roosevelt once lived.

The author also makes grateful acknowledgment to the following for permission to reprint quotations included in this book:

Harper & Brothers for quotations from *Bill Sewall's Life of T.R.* by William Wingate Sewell; *The Boys' Life of Theodore Roosevelt* by Hermann Hagedorn; and *This Is My Story* by Eleanor Roosevelt.

Harvard University Press for quotations from Volume I of *Letters of Theodore Roosevelt,* edited by Elting E. Morison.

Mrs. Alice Roosevelt Longworth for brief quotations from *Private Diaries* of Theodore Roosevelt, now in the Manuscript Division of the Library of Congress.

Charles Scribner's Sons for quotations from *Diaries of Boyhood and Youth* by Theodore Roosevelt; *Letters from Theodore Roosevelt to Anna Roosevelt Cowles; My Brother, Theodore Roosevelt* by Corinne Robinson; and Theodore Roosevelt's *Autobiography.*

University of Oklahoma Press for quotations from *A Front Row Seat* by Nicholas Roosevelt.

Frances Cavanah

Washington, D. C.

1

A MORNING BREEZE rumpled his fair hair as Theodore Roosevelt, Jr. turned into Broadway to buy some strawberries. The strawberries were for the family breakfast, and his mother had told him to hurry back. When he reached the fish market, he stopped. There, on a wooden slab, lay the body of a big, sleek, glistening animal. The round smooth body was covered with short oily hair. It had flippers instead of legs. Its ears were very small and its whiskers very long.

"It's a seal," said Theodore, his voice rising in excitement. "Where did it come from?"

"A fisherman caught it in the harbor," the owner of the market replied. "A big fish, isn't it?"

"A seal isn't a fish," Theodore informed him. "It's an animal."

"You don't mean to tell me! Now, Master Theodore, how did you know that?" asked the man. This pale, thin boy with the pipestem legs was always saying the most surprising things. Yet he couldn't be much over seven.

"I've read about seals in my books," Theodore answered easily. "I've seen pictures of them."

"All I know," said the owner stubbornly, "is that seal meat fetches a fancy price."

"You're not going to sell it?" asked Theodore.

"Of course. What else? Seal meat is mighty tasty."

The boy stared wistfully at the seal. He wished that he could buy it, but not to eat. He wanted to take it home and learn how to preserve it the way animals are preserved in a museum. "I have to go now," he said, "but I'll be back."

When he returned that afternoon, he took a folding rule from his pocket. He measured the long body from the tip of its black nose to the end of its sleek, black tail. He measured it across. Then he jotted down some figures on a piece of paper. This was what he thought a naturalist—a man who studies animals and plants—would do. He came again the next day, and the next day after that, just to look at the seal, but each time there was less of it to see. Customers had been buying slices of seal meat to take home and cook. Soon only the skull was left.

"Take it, if you want it," said the owner good-naturedly.

Never had Theodore felt so proud as he did that spring day in 1866 when he turned into Twentieth Street in New York City. He was carrying his trophy carefully in both hands, as he climbed the steps to the high front door of his house and stepped into the hall. To the left was the parlor, very elegant and formal, with stiff high-backed chairs and an elaborate gas chandelier. Theodore liked the way the hundreds of tiny cut-glass prisms sparkled in the dim light that filtered through the white lace curtains, but he did not take time to stop and admire them. He could hear voices coming from the nursery on the third floor, and he rushed upstairs. He was breathing hard when he opened the door.

"See what I have," he shouted.

His little sister Corinne and her chum, Edith Carow, looked up from their game of dolls. Elliott was showing his new tin soldiers to two visiting cousins, Jimmie and Johnnie Roosevelt.

"What is it, Teedie?" Jimmie asked

"It is the head of a seal—a real skeleton," Theodore replied. "I'm going to add it to my collection. Why don't we start a museum?"

"Ugh!" Edie wrinkled up her pretty little nose at the sight of the dead seal. Then she and Conie turned back to their dolls. Ellie, a neat little boy of six, began to put his tin soldiers away in their box. But the two cousins, who were about Teedie's age, were caught up in his enthusiasm, and they followed him into his room. On his dresser, beside his brush and comb, they saw an old abandoned bird's nest. Rocks and stones were piled on the table. Beside them, in a cage, two white mice blinked black, beady eyes.

"What are we going to call our museum?" Jimmie asked.

Teedie screwed up his face, trying to think. His father had been talking with some of his friends about starting a museum in New York City. One name that had been suggested was "The American Museum of Natural History."

"We might call our collection the *Roosevelt* Museum of Natural History," said Teedie. "Of course, it won't be as big as Father's museum, but we can find a lot of things for it."

Although Theodore was often ill with asthma, he worked hard on his collection. He and his cousins continued to add to it for several years. Once when Teedie's parents were visiting relatives in Georgia, he sent them long letters, telling them exactly what he wanted. He asked his father to bring him specimens of a plant called supplejacks. He asked his mother to visit some battlefield of the War Between the States, and find some trophies.

His mother wrote to him about the good times she was having with her friends in the town where she had lived as a girl. Her room at the hotel was filled with flowers. "My mouth opened with astonishment," he replied, "when I heard how many flowers were sent in to you. I could revel in the buggie ones. I jumped with delight when I found you heard a mocking-bird. Get some of its feathers if you can."

Teedie's father had given him several good scientific books, and he never tired of reading them. He even wrote a book which he called *Natural History of Insects.* He wrote it out by hand in a note-book. "All the insects that I write about," he said on the first page, "inhabbit North America. Now and then a friend has told me something about them, but mostly I have gained their habits from ofserv-a-tion."

Two of the words were not spelled correctly, but Teedie knew what they meant. His own powers of observation were very good indeed. When he began to keep a diary, he wrote about many of the interesting things he saw in nature.

One day he found a litter of white mice and put them in his mother's ice box where he thought they would be safe. The next morning when he returned for them, they were gone. His lovely mother—his "little Motherling" as he often called her—had thrown them out. She tried to explain that no good housekeeper likes mice in her ice box, but Teedie would not listen.

"What hurts me," he sputtered angrily, "is the loss to science."

His mother turned away to hide a smile, but only for a minute. "There is something else," she said sternly. "The upstairs maid tells me that your room is a disgrace, with all those birds' nests and rocks and live animals you keep up there. She refuses to clean it another day. I'm afraid that your museum will have to go."

Teedie could hardly believe what he heard. How could she ask him to give up the collection on which he had worked so hard? His breath came in gasps, and Mrs. Roosevelt looked down at him in dismay. He was so brave about his illness that it was hard to scold him. He turned and ran up to his room.

By supper time he felt better. This was the evening to which he had been looking forward. His father had promised to take the children to see Miss Satterie's night school for boys and girls whose parents had recently arrived from Italy. Because the elder Roosevelt was well-to-do, he felt it his duty—as it was his pleasure—to help others who were less fortunate. He was one of the founders of the Children's Aid Society which managed both the school and the Newsboys' Lodging House, and he not only gave them money but visited them regularly.

Daniel, the coachman, had the carriage ready and waiting in front of the brownstone front house where Teedie lived. The four horses—called a "four-in-hand"—pawed the cobblestones impatiently, as Mr. Roosevelt climbed into the high driver's seat and picked up the reins. Behind him were two lower seats, facing each other. His wife and older daughter Anna, or Bamie, sat in one, the three younger children in the other. And then they were off, dashing between rows of houses which looked much like their own. There were no high buildings in New York in those days. The church spires, silhouetted against the darkening sky, were taller than any of the houses.

Finally Mr. Roosevelt turned into a narrow street in the poorer section of the city. Here houses called tenements huddled close together, and he pulled the horses to a stop before Miss Satterie's school.

"Signore Roosevelt! Signore Roosevelt!" her pupils shouted, as they gathered around him, talking in a mixture of English and Italian.

Teedie drew close to his mother. He was not used to playing with children outside his own family, and he felt shy. He also felt a warm glow of pride. His father was so good, so kind, so strong.

By the time the family returned home, Theodore was very tired. He went to sleep propped up on pillows, so he could breathe more easily. A few hours later he awoke, wheezing and coughing. There seemed to be an iron band around his chest. Another attack of asthma! he thought fretfully. He seldom went ten days without one.

This asthma was always interfering with what he wanted to do. Because of it, he could not go to school like other boys. When he was younger, Bamie and his Aunt Annie had given him lessons, and now

11

he had a tutor. Being at home so much had one advantage. He had more time to read, and he liked to imagine himself having the same adventures as did the heroes in his books. This often helped him forget how ill he felt.

But not tonight! The band around his chest grew tighter. He was choking. He thought only of trying to breathe, of trying to get a single breath of air.

In the darkness he heard a door open. There was the sputter of a match, as someone lighted the gas jet on the wall. A kind, grave face was leaning over the bed. "Teedie," his father said, "we're going for a drive in the country. Perhaps getting outdoors will help."

He wrapped a blanket around his son, carried him downstairs, and lifted him into the trap, a smaller carriage, drawn by a single horse. New York was strangely quiet at that hour. The striking of the horses' hoofs on the cobblestones was the only sound in the still night air. They drove up Broadway to Fifty-first Street, where it became Bloomingdale Road. And then they were in the country—the blessed, blessed country. Teedie drew a deep breath. If only he could stay outdoors all of the time, outdoors where he could breathe!

"Do you feel better, son?"

The boy nodded, leaning his head against his father's shoulder. He still did not trust himself to speak, afraid that he would start coughing again. But he *did* feel better, and by the time dawn broke, he was breathing evenly. His father turned back toward the city.

"Your mother and I have been wondering," he said, "what to do about your museum."

Teedie's heart sank.

"We cannot blame the maid," Mr. Roosevelt went on. "It *is* hard to clean your room. Would you like to move the Roosevelt Museum to the third floor? There is an empty bookcase up there where you can keep your collection, and it won't be in anybody's way."

A smile spread over the boy's thin features. He should have realized that his father would think of something.

"Do you know what I want to be when I grow up?" he asked in a sudden burst of confidence. "I want to be a naturalist."

"Well, son, that is a good ambition," said Mr. Roosevelt.

Teedie sat up straight. "Don't you think I *can* be a naturalist?" he asked.

"You have the mind, Theodore," his father replied. "But you don't have the body, and without the body the mind cannot go as far as it should. The doctors have not been able to help much, and there is only one thing left to do. You yourself must *make* your body."

"How, Father?"

"By building up your strength. You can start by going on long walks, and then I want you to take regular exercises. You must take them every day. You may grow tired of them after the first few times. It is drudgery, very hard work indeed, to make your body, but I know that you can do it."

Theodore thought of the heroes that he liked to read about in books. None of them had asthma. He wanted to be strong and brave like them; most of all he wanted to be like his father. He gritted his teeth and threw back his head defiantly.

"I'll do it," he said. "I promise. I'll *make* my body."

2

M<small>R.</small> R<small>OOSEVELT</small> took his family to the country every summer, and
several months each year were spent at some cottage near the Hudson
River. Jimmie and Johnnie Roosevelt often joined them, and two
other young cousins, Maud and John Elliott, came up from Savannah,
Georgia, for long visits. The children ran barefoot, climbed trees,
watched the haying and harvesting, picked apples, and gathered
nuts. They stained their faces with pokeberry juice and pretended
they were Indians.

Best of all, in the country, they could have as many pets as they
wanted—dogs, cats, rabbits, turtles, squirrels, guinea pigs, and horses.
Pony Grant was their favorite. He had a strange habit: when first
mounted, he would toss the rider over his head. The rider would
pick himself up, dust himself off, and mount again. Usually the pony

14

made no further objection. He had had his fun, and would lope off gently through the country lanes.

The shaggy little horse had been named for a famous Union general, but Conie did not know that. When Ulysses S. Grant was nominated for President of the United States in the summer of 1868, Conie was puzzled. "Was he named after our pony?" she asked.

"By jove," said Teedie, "the general wasn't named after our pony. Our pony was named after him."

"Oh!" said Conie.

Teedie made a sound that his mother once described as "a sharp ungreased squeak." She said that his squeaks almost crushed her eardrum, but she was glad that he felt like laughing. He had been having asthma again.

After the family's return to the house on Twentieth Street, Mr. Roosevelt carried out the plan that he hoped would build up Teedie's strength. There was the sound of sawing and hammering on the third floor, as carpenters turned the porch off the nursery into a gymnasium. Against the wall of the house, there was a rack in which dumbbells and Indian clubs were kept. Jimmie Roosevelt was as interested as Teedie in the trapeze, and Ellie soon learned to hit the punching bag with well-aimed blows. Conie and Edie preferred the seesaw.

Teedie used the gymnasium every day. In order to widen his chest, he chinned himself between two bars. He pulled himself up and down, up and down—again and *again*. It was very boring, until he found a way to make his exercises more interesting.

One morning his mother was in the back yard, when she heard laughter above. She looked up, and her heart seemed to freeze. A railing had been built on the porch for the protection of the children, but on top of that railing the seesaw had now been placed. She could not see the boy on the porch. But the boy on the end overhanging the yard three stories below was Theodore Roosevelt, Jr.

Mrs. Roosevelt did not dare to call out. She feared that if her son were taken by surprise, he might lose his balance and fall.

15

She rushed into the house and up two flights of stairs. When she reached the door leading to the third-floor porch, Jimmie and Teedie were still teeter-tottering back and forth. They were safe, but for how long? Jimmie's end of the seesaw was on the floor. Teedie at his end was high in the air.

"Jimmie," she said trying to keep the quaver out of her voice, "stay where you are. Don't move. I'll help to hold this end of the seesaw steady. Now, Teedie—" she took a deep breath—"slide down toward me—very, very *carefully*—very, very *slowly*—"

Teedie blinked at her nearsightedly. At this distance her face was only a blur, but he could hear her. There was no mistaking the firmness in her voice. He knew that he must obey.

"Don't hurry," she went on, in that same low tone. "Come slowly—carefully—"

A moment later Teedie was in her arms. She did not know whether to hug or to scold him, but she was so relieved that she decided to hug him. Then she burst into tears, which made Theodore feel worse than a scolding would have. He kissed his mother and promised never to do anything like that again.

On her way downstairs Mrs. Roosevelt dried her eyes. Was Teedie really any better? He was still so pale; were the exercises really helping? Teedie often wondered the same thing, but he knew that his father was right. Unless he became husky and strong, he could never be a naturalist.

By the time he was thirteen, he had decided to specialize in birds. He read everything he could about them. He pored over pictures of birds in books by the great artist and naturalist, John James Audubon. One day, in a musty little shop near his home, he met a man who had known Audubon many years before. Mr. Bell, now a white-haired old gentleman, was a taxidermist. He knew how to preserve birds that had been shot, so that they looked almost alive.

"Do you think I could learn taxidermy, Mr. Bell?" asked Teedie.

"Of course," was the reply, "but it will be hard work."

Teedie did not mind work. He took lessons from Mr. Bell, and the next summer when his family went to the country he asked for a gun. His plan was to collect birds of a number of different kinds, or species. After he shot them, he would preserve them, the way Mr. Bell did, and keep them in his museum. His father bought the gun and showed Teedie how to use it.

It was a proud boy who started out to hunt with his cousins the next day, but he soon realized that something was wrong. Jimmie and Johnnie could shoot down birds that Teedie had not even seen. On the way home, they passed a billboard. There were words on it, but to him they were only a blur. They all ran together.

Jimmie, however, read the words out loud.

Teedie was frightened. As soon as he reached home, he went to his father. "I couldn't even see the letters," he explained.

"Why, son," said Mr. Roosevelt, "you must be nearsighted. Why didn't you tell me before? We'll have to get you some spectacles."

They made a special trip to the city to see an oculist, who examined Teedie's eyes and promised to give him spectacles that would help. Theodore was disappointed when he found that he would have to wait for them. The oculist explained that the lenses must be ground especially for him, and this would take time.

That night he woke up with another attack of asthma. The next day he was so tired that he did not even want to go hunting with his cousins. He did not want to play Indians with Ellie and Conie, or even to ride Pony Grant. He just lay back, propped up with pillows in a big chair, and thought about the heroes in his books.

He pretended that he was Daniel Boone crossing the mountains.

Then he was Davy Crockett, fighting in defense of the Alamo.

Later he was one of George Washington's soldiers at Valley Forge. He was hungry and shivering with the cold, but he did not complain. In his imagination, he was very, very brave.

His father came in and sat beside him. "Son," said Mr. Roosevelt, "how would you like to go up to Maine? To Moosehead Lake?"

"All of us?"

"No, just you. Perhaps you will find it easier to breathe up there in the crisp, dry air."

"Can't Ellie go with me?" Although Teedie was a year and a half older, he had grown used to depending on his husky younger brother.

"No," his father replied, "Ellie does not need to go, and you do. You will be fourteen in October—quite old enough to travel alone."

The last part of the journey to Moosehead Lake was made by stagecoach. Across from Teedie sat two boys about his age, but much taller and with strong, broad shoulders. The sight of Theodore, thin and pale, seemed to amuse them.

"Look at the pipestems," one of them said, pointing to Theodore's legs.

Theodore swallowed hard. He was already painfully conscious of his long, thin legs.

"Pipestems! Pipestems!" his two companions began to chant. "Look at his pipestems, will you?"

At first Theodore looked out of the window and pretended not to hear, but the boys went right on teasing. He stood it as long as he could. Then one of his tormentors called him "Sissy."

"Take that back," he said.

"What if I don't? What will you do about it?"

"Yes, what will the nice little sissy do?" the second boy added in a mocking tone.

Teedie doubled up his fists. "I—I—I'll show you," he said.

At that moment the driver of the stagecoach brought his horses to a halt. He wanted to give them water. The two bigger boys got out. They looked back at Theodore.

"Well, come on and show us. Are you a scaredy-cat?"

Theodore reluctantly climbed from the coach. He had never been in a fight. Ellie had always been strong enough to protect both of them from bullies, but now Elliott was several hundred miles away. Theodore was alone. Again he doubled up his fists and lunged toward

18

the taller of the two boys. The next instant he felt a sharp sting on the side of his face, and he was lying on his back.

Not quite sure how it had happened, he struggled to his feet. The second boy stood before him, waving his fists and grinning. Teedie lunged again. A long arm shot out, and he felt himself being shaken back and forth. He was being shaken as a cat might shake a mouse.

"Stop it, boys," the stagecoach driver called. "Don't hurt the little fellow."

The three boys got back into the coach. Teedie had not been really hurt, except for his pride. His face was burning with shame.

At Moosehead Lake he had plenty of time to think over what had happened. It must never happen again, he told himself fiercely. Next time he must be able to defend himself. When he returned home, he had another talk with his father.

"I wish I could take boxing lessons," he said.

Mr. Roosevelt nodded approvingly. "A good idea! There is no better way to make yourself physically fit. I shall hire John Long to teach you. He used to be a prizefighter. You will have several weeks to train with him before we sail."

"Oh, not another terrible trip to Europe?" Teedie protested. His father had taken the family abroad once before, and the children had been homesick. They had grown very tired of sightseeing.

"The last trip was three years ago," said Mr. Roosevelt, "and you were too young to appreciate what you saw. Anyway Egypt is different from Europe, and it has a mild dry climate that may help your asthma."

"Are there birds in Egypt?" Teedie asked.

"Of course. You'll probably see a number of new species—many different kinds of birds from the ones we have here."

"All right," the boy went on more cheerfully, "I can add some birds, hundreds of them maybe, to my collection. I'll be able to shoot better after I get my spectacles."

The spectacles were delivered a short time before the Roosevelts were to sail in the fall of 1872. They had very thick lenses, and Teedie was astonished the first time he wore them. The trees were no longer a blur of green, with smaller blurs of gold or scarlet. It was early October and the leaves were beginning to turn. The wonder of it was that he could see each separate leaf, shining in the sunlight. He walked over to a bed of dahlias—and the dahlias had petals! He glanced at the sky. How strange he had never known that clouds were so soft and fluffy! Then he heard the cardinal. It was perched on a branch and he could see it, even at a distance. He could actually see its exquisite feathers. He smiled up at his father.

"I had no idea how beautiful the world is," he said.

3

The family had gathered on the deck of a ship crossing the Mediterranean Sea, and Teedie was again grateful for his new spectacles. As he peered through the mist, eager for his first glimpse of the Egyptian shoreline, the lighthouse in the harbor of Alexandria came into view. It was more than two thousand years old, and taller than any building the children had ever seen.

"Alexandria! How I gazed on it!" Theodore wrote in his diary. "It was Egypt, the most ancient of all countries. It was a sight to awaken a thousand thoughts, and it did."

Theodore liked to use colorful words, and he soon found he was going to need them really to describe his travels. From Alexandria, the family took a train for Cairo, where Mr. Roosevelt rented a *dahabeah,* an Egyptian houseboat. There was a comfortable deck shaded by awnings and, inside, a salon or big room where the family ate their meals. They slept in the staterooms below.

Luckily for the others, Theodore had a stateroom to himself, for he had brought his taxidermy outfit. On his table he placed a book on Egyptian birds and a little box of labels. He was proud of those labels. The words "Roosevelt Museum of Natural History" were printed on them in red ink. Johnnie and Jimmie Roosevelt had given them to him before he sailed, and it had been decided that he was to bring back as many specimens as possible for their museum.

Two weeks before Christmas 1872, the Roosevelts began their journey up the Nile River. How different it was from December in New York! The hot sun beat down. The sky was very blue, the river very green. Once a year it overflowed its banks, and when the waters receded they left behind a wide strip of fertile soil on both sides. Tall, stately date palms grew on these lush green strips of land, and it was here that the farmers planted their crops. Farther back from the river lay the sands of the great Sahara Desert, sometimes flat, sometimes rising in high cliffs. Cream-colored in the early morning, they deepened to gold as the sun rose in the sky.

The family did most of their traveling by night, and nearly every morning the sailors would tie up the boat along the shore. Then Mr. Roosevelt would rent donkeys, and set out with his wife and children to explore some interesting old ruin or temple. Teedie's favorite temple was at Karnak, near Thebes, once the capital of Egypt.

"We saw it by moonlight," he said in a letter to his Aunt Annie. "To wander among those great columns under the same moon that had looked down on them for thousands of years was awe-inspiring."

Teedie's health seemed better, and scarcely a day passed that he did not go shooting with his father. "I have procured between one and two hundred skins," Teedie wrote his Aunt Annie; then added, "The sport is injurious to my trousers."

During the three months on the Nile, Teedie had suddenly

started to grow. His trousers were too short, his coat too tight, but he did not seem to care how he looked. He forgot to comb his hair. He forgot to wash his hands, which were usually stained with chemicals. His shoes were muddy. He was as grubby as Ellie was neat.

"Ah, Teedie," said Mrs. Roosevelt, "I can hardly wait to get back to Cairo where we can buy you some new clothes."

After leaving Egypt the Roosevelts visited the Holy Land. By April 1873, they had reached Constantinople, in Turkey. "I think I have enjoyed myself more this winter than I ever did before," Teedie wrote Conie's friend, Edith Carow. "I think I enjoyed Egypt most."

Teedie could look back on the winter with much satisfaction. He had several hundred stuffed birds to take back to the Roosevelt Museum of Natural History, but unfortunately his old enemy asthma had returned. Another disappointment came when the family reached Vienna. Mr. Roosevelt announced that he must go back to New York.

"Can't we go home with you, Father?" Conie asked.

Her father shook his head. "Not yet, Conie. Your mother and Bamie are going to stay in Europe for a while longer. You and the boys will go to Germany. To Dresden."

Ellie looked pleased. John and Maud Elliott were living with their mother in Dresden. It would be fun to see their cousins again. "Will we live with John and Maud?" asked Ellie.

"No, son. You are to spend the summer with the family of Herr Doktor Minkwitz. He is a fine, cultured gentleman, and his daughter, Fräulein Anna, will give you lessons. You children have had your holiday. Now it is time for some good, hard study."

The young Roosevelts soon learned to love Dresden with its copper-green roofs and tall church spires rising against a background of vine-covered hills. They liked the Herr Doktor who, as a young man, had fought in the German Revolution of 1848. Now that he was older, he was as grave and dignified as his wife, Frau Minkwitz, was hearty and good-natured. Their eldest daughter, Fräulein Anna, was a good teacher, and Teedie became so interested that he asked her to give him longer lessons. Ellie, not to be outdone by his brother, asked for longer lessons, too.

Sunday afternoons were usually spent with their Aunt Lucy Elliott who lived close by. John and Maud Elliott and the three young Roosevelts decided to form "The Dresden Literary American Club" with a secret motto, "W.A.N.A." Only the members knew that those mysterious letters stood for the words, "We are no asses." They had a great deal of fun over that motto, but their club had a serious purpose. At each meeting they read the stories and poems they had written during the week.

Teedie's chief hobby, as always, was natural history. He took long walks through the fields and forests near Dresden. He watched butterflies fluttering by the wayside and listened to the birds trilling in the woods. Once a doe and her fawn bounded across his path. Frequently he returned from a walk carrying a snake or a hedgehog or some other small animal. These "specimens" had a habit of escaping from partly opened bureau drawers, to the dismay of Fräulein Anna and her mother.

"My scientific pursuits," he admitted in a letter to his Aunt Annie, "cause the family a good deal of consternation."

When Maud Elliott, aged twelve, heard about this, she decided to make Teedie the hero of a story, and she read it before the Dresden Literary American Club. "Well, my dear little friends," she began, "I must tell you something about Theodore. You know he was a naturalist on a small scale—"

Conie and Ellie giggled. John said, "Sh!" Maud frowned, and everyone became quiet.

"He was a very amusing boy," she went on, "but he had a great fault. He was very absentminded, so much so that whenever his mother would tell him to go and do something for her he would say 'O yes you pretty little thing,' but instead of doing it directly he would go and skin his birds or something that he took it into his head to skin—"

By this time everyone was laughing.

"And then," Maud finished, emphasizing each word, "he always thought that he could do things better than anyone else."

Theodore blushed, but he knew how to take a joke, even on himself. He made up his mind that *he* would write a funny story for the next meeting. He stood up and announced his subject: "Mrs. Field Mouse's Dinner Party."

There was a groan. Teedie *would* write about a mouse, the other members declared.

After hearing the first sentence, they realized that they had been mistaken. True, the main characters in the story were named Mr. and Mrs. Mouse. Among the other characters were Mrs. Frog,

Mrs. Bullfrog, Miss Katydid, and Sir Grasshopper. But the animals in Teedie's story were really people in disguise.

He tried hard to keep his face straight as he read:

"'My Dear,' said Mrs. M. to Mr. M. one day as they were sitting on an elegant acorn sofa, just before breakfast, 'My Dear, I think that we must really give a dinner party.'"

The story went on and on. Mrs. Mouse was trying very hard to impress her guests. Her guests—like certain silly people in New York—were trying to impress one another, and Theodore was secretly pleased by the laughter and applause. He had proved that he could be funny, too.

When he tried to talk in German, his audience was not always so appreciative. One day he was telling Emily, the servant girl, about a book he had read about the western part of the United States. He said that the cowboys used a lasso to catch their horses, but Emily did not know what a lasso was. He explained that it was a long rope with a loop at the end, and the loop became tighter when the rope was pulled. As he struggled to find the right German words, Emily became more and more confused. Theodore almost exploded with impatience.

"Here, I'll show you," he said in English, which she did not understand at all.

He took a big towel and threw it over Emily's head. The terrified girl began to scream, and the entire family came running.

"What is wrong?" asked Herr Doktor sternly. "What have you been doing, Theodore?"

"Nothing," Theodore replied. "I only wanted to show Emily how a lasso is used."

Frau Minkwitz put her arm around his shoulders. She had grown to love this noisy boy, and she knew that he meant no harm. He was too kind to frighten anyone on purpose.

Fräulein Anna was also very fond of him. After a few weeks of lessons, she decided that he was a remarkable student. Several times she had long talks with Mrs. Roosevelt who often came to Dresden to visit her sons and little daughter. Much as Theodore's beautiful mother loved him, she was worried. She knew that his habit of bringing home "specimens" must be hard on the German family.

"I wonder what is going to become of my Teedie," she said.

"You need not be anxious about him," Fräulein Anna assured her. "One day he may be a great professor. Why, he may even become President of the United States."

"Whatever gave you that idea?" asked Mrs. Roosevelt.

And then she smiled. Anna had probably heard the old saying that every American boy has a chance to become President. Anna did not smile. She had a feeling that she had not heard the last of Theodore Roosevelt.

Soon afterwards Mrs. Roosevelt took Fräulein and the children for a holiday in Switzerland. By this time, Theodore had started a collection of stones, and he spent most of his time gathering them. The day they left their inn in one town, a man servant carried Theodore's trunk out to the wagon that was to haul the luggage to the railroad station. The trunk seemed heavy. Mrs. Roosevelt, Bamie, and the younger children entered the waiting carriage. The coachman raised his whip.

At that moment there was a cry of "Wait! Wait!"

The same servant stood in the doorway of the inn. In his arms he held a large bundle of clothing—suits, underwear, shoes, and stockings—and it all belonged to Theodore.

"Teedie," said his mother, "what does this mean?"

She did not wait for an explanation, but asked the servant to open the trunk. It was filled with stones. Teedie had thrown his clothes out to make room for them. At her order, the stones were thrown out, and the servant hurriedly packed the boy's clothes. There was a look of pain on Teedie's face. He jumped down out of the carriage and filled his pockets with stones. But most of his precious collection had to be left behind.

He said nothing. He knew that he had sorely tried his mother's patience. Anyway, it had been a wonderful holiday!

He was glad that he had it to remember. After he returned to Dresden and his mother had departed, he was ill again. "Dearest Motherling," he wrote her, "picture to yourself an antiquated woodchuck with his cheeks filled with nuts . . . and a cloth resembling a castoff stocking around his head; picture to yourself that, I say, and you will have a good likeness of your hopeful offspring while suffering from mumps."

Luckily Theodore's sense of humor helped him, not only through mumps, but through several severe attacks of asthma. He wrote his father that he could not "speak without blowing like an abridged hippopotamus." It was easier not to talk at all, and he found comfort in his books. By now he knew German well enough to read the great epic poem about Siegfried, and he thrilled to the old tale.

Oh, to be strong like Siegfried! he thought. The hero of the German legend had conquered a dragon. He, Theodore Roosevelt, Jr., had asthma to conquer. In one way, the asthma was a more difficult enemy because it kept coming back, and he knew that he must try even harder to build up his strength. He *must*—if he was ever to be like the heroes he admired.

He looked into the mirror. A tall, puny boy, too thin and much too pale, looked back at him. But the boy was thrusting out his chin.

4

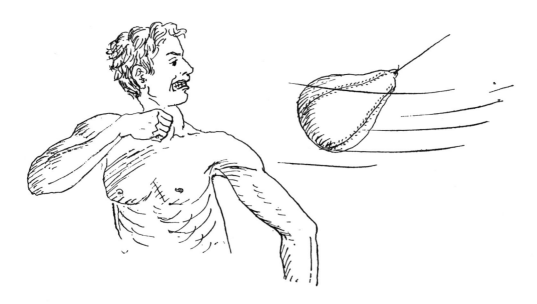

THEODORE'S FIFTEENTH birthday was spent on board the steamship *Russia,* which was bringing the children and their mother home. When they reached New York early in November 1873, Mr. Roosevelt welcomed them to a new house on Fifty-seventh Street. One room had already been turned into a gymnasium. Even before Teedie unpacked, he began to chin himself on the trapeze.

"The year abroad did you good," said his father. "But you still have asthma, son."

A shadow crossed Teedie's face.

"Father," he said earnestly, "I am coming here every day to exercise. Then may I take some more lessons with Mr. Long?"

"More boxing lessons?"

Teedie nodded. He had practiced boxing with Elliott, while

they were in Dresden, but he had to admit that he wasn't very good.

"All right," Mr. Roosevelt went on. "We'll see John Long tomorrow. We also must find you a tutor. It is time to think about college. You want to go to Harvard, don't you?"

"Yes, Father, I do. Only—" Teedie hesitated. He wished that he could attend a "prep" or preparatory school with his friends.

Mr. Roosevelt seemed to read his thoughts. "You are not strong enough to go to school, not just yet. It will be better for you to have lessons at home. You must concentrate on studying hard, as well as on building your strength."

Because Teedie had been ill so much, his education had been uneven. He had read more than most boys of his age, and he was far ahead of them in his knowledge of history, literature, and science. In arithmetic he was far behind, and his spelling was terrible. After Arthur Cutler, the new tutor, arrived, there were daily lessons in languages and mathematics. Teedie already knew some French and German, but he found Latin dull. Mathematics made him yawn. How much more interesting it was to wander through the woods, collecting new specimens for his museum.

Arthur Cutler was patient but firm. He explained that any boy who hoped to go to Harvard must pass an examination in both subjects. Theodore Roosevelt gritted his teeth and set to work.

The boxing lessons were almost as hard. John Long expected a great deal of his pupils. On the walls of his room were the pictures of prize fighters he had known, their gloved hands upraised as they faced one another in the ring. They looked so husky! The other pupils were husky, and Theodore dreaded the time when he would have to box with them. He knew that Elliott had never hit him as hard as these strangers would. How could he go into the ring to practice with these bigger, stronger boys?

And then he remembered a book he had been reading by Frederick Marryat, one of his favorite authors. The hero was a young midshipman, on a British man-of-war, who was terrified at the thought of going into battle. His captain told him that nearly all new sailors are frightened, but those who act as though they are *not* afraid learn to overcome their fear. By pretending to be brave, they actually *become* brave.

"I'll try it," Theodore said to himself as he swaggered across the floor. He looked at the punching bag, which hung from the ceiling. Never had it looked so big. But he stuck out his jaw. He bared his teeth, to make himself look fierce. He drew back his arm. He doubled his hand into a fist. With every ounce of strength that he could muster, he let go with a mighty blow. Under the impact of that blow, the punching bag swung several feet away from him. And then it swung back. He dodged it just in time.

Why, it was easier than he had thought—this business of pretending not to be afraid! Hour after hour, he banged away at the big punching bag. He chinned himself on the trapeze. He jumped rope to strengthen the muscles in his legs. Then one day Mr. Long announced there was to be a series of boxing matches, and Theodore was to take part in one of them. He and two other pupils about the same weight were to try for the "lightweight" championship. The winner would receive a pewter cup.

If only he could win it! thought Theodore. He wanted to prove to his father that he was getting stronger. He wanted to prove it to the other boys. Most of all, he wanted to prove it to himself.

The afternoon of the match he laid aside his glasses and put on his boxing gloves. He stepped out on the mat and faced his first opponent. The two boys waited for the starting gong. The winner would have to fight the third boy. That second fight would decide the championship.

Theodore flexed his muscles and thrust out his chin. He was trying to act brave, and suddenly he *felt* brave. When the starting gong sounded, he led with a left jab at his opponent. The opponent dodged and came back with a right-hand body blow that sent Theodore sprawling on the mat. The breath was knocked out of him, and he

31

could hear the referee counting: "One—two—three—four—five—"

With an effort, he staggered to his feet. The next round was a draw, and the next one after that. Each fighter was trying to hit the other one, while, at the same time, trying to protect himself from being hit. In the sixth round Theodore raised his right hand. It looked as though he intended to aim a blow at his opponent's head. The opponent raised his hand to ward off the blow, and Theodore saw his chance. Out shot his left hand and hit the other boy squarely in the chest. Caught off guard, he sprawled on the mat.

The referee stood over him and began to count. He counted to ten. The boy did not get up. Theodore had won.

The first match was over, but there was a second match. Theodore won that, too. The referee came forward, lifted his left hand, and made an announcement: "Theodore Roosevelt, the lightweight champion," he said.

When the "champion" reached his room, he was carrying the pewter cup that he had won as a prize. Proudly he placed it on his bookcase. He wished that those boys who had trounced him on the way to Moosehead Lake could see it!

5

Living on Fifty-seventh Street had many advantages. At that time this section of the city seemed more like a small town. Close by was Central Park where the young Roosevelts and their numerous cousins and friends had picnics and rode horseback. In the winter, they went skating on the frozen pond. Mrs. Roosevelt organized a dancing class for them. Teedie was not a good dancer, but he tried. Sometimes he danced with Edith Carow who, at twelve, was prettier than ever. He also danced with another friend of Conie's, Fanny Smith.

Fanny decided that Theodore was overcoming his shyness, now that he was growing up, but sometimes he embarrassed her. When she sat next to him at a formal dinner party, he kept whispering funny remarks. The other guests began to stare. No one but Theodore—and he kept his face straight—knew why she was shaking with laughter. She laughed so hard that she was afraid she would have to leave the room.

"He is such fun; the most original boy I ever knew," she wrote in her diary.

When the young people came to the house on Fifty-seventh Street, Theodore Roosevelt, Sr. frequently joined them. He helped them to plan amateur theatricals. Some of the plays they gave were amusing; others were serious. They never knew quite what to expect of Mr. Roosevelt. On the spur of the moment, he might ask first one, then another, to make a speech. Then that boy or girl would have to stand up and talk about any subject that was suggested. He also encouraged them to read aloud. There were always good books to choose from in the library.

"Under the trees, before the fire, or riding through the woods," said Fanny, "we would discuss our favorites."

Several of Mr. Roosevelt's relatives lived on Long Island for part of each year. Their summer homes were near the village of Oyster Bay, and the family of Theodore, Sr. was overjoyed when he rented a place close by. The big white house with its four tall columns was called "Tranquillity," a name that was a joke to their friends.

"Anything less tranquil than that happy home cannot be imagined," said Conie in a book that she wrote years later. "Endless young cousins and friends shared the delightful life we led in that enchanted spot."

The next three summers were among the happiest in Theodore's life. He spent three hours a day with his tutor, but that was less than half the time he gave to study during the rest of the year. The golden weeks at Oyster Bay were filled with fun. Nearly every afternoon he had a ride on Lightfoot, his horse. His father took the boys on over-night camping trips, and he and his cousin Jimmie (who was now known as West Roosevelt) went on long cross-country walks. Often Theodore roamed through the deep woods alone, pausing to study a flower or to listen to the call of a bird. His old habits persisted, and he brought many specimens back to the room he shared with Elliott.

Ellie tried to be patient. But the day he found a snake under his bed, he decided something had to be done. He took a piece of chalk and drew a white line down the center of the floor.

"You stay on your side of this line, and I'll stay on mine," he announced firmly.

No one—not even the long-suffering Elliott—could be angry with Teedie for very long. Fanny, who came to visit every summer, always remembered his gaiety. "This quality," she said, "was a noticeable family trait, but in Theodore it seemed to reach its height."

Another visitor, who was almost like a member of the family, was Edith Carow. Theodore took her rowing on Long Island Sound, and they laughed together as the boat plowed through the choppy water. Sometimes they gathered wild flowers in the woods. Both liked to read, and they liked many of the same books. Although Edith was three years younger than Theodore, she seemed the older of the two. She was as calm as he was excitable. He called her "Her Ladyship," just to tease, but she was the sort of girl that he could talk to about almost anything.

One day, as they sat on his favorite hill, he told her of his hopes and plans for college. In the middle of a sentence, he paused. The birds were twittering in the trees. He pulled a notebook from his pocket and wrote the notes of a bird call he had not heard before. There was a long, comfortable silence. Edith, looking down through a network of leaves, could see the waters of the Sound shimmering in the sunlight. The Connecticut shore was a dim blue line in the distance.

"How peaceful it is here," she said dreamily.

"It wasn't always peaceful," Theodore replied, his blue eyes lighting with interest. "It was on this very hilltop that some of the old Indian chiefs used to hold their war councils. There was one, Chief Sagamore Mohannis, whose tribe once owned all of this land. They signed a treaty with the white man and gave the land away two and a half centuries ago. Just think, Edith—two hundred and fifty years ago."

How much had happened since then, he thought.

And what was to happen next? he wondered. What was to happen to him? He wanted to enter Harvard, but would he be accepted? He had worked hard since his return from Egypt, and he continued to work hard during the next winter. In June 1876, only two and a half years after he began to study with Mr. Cutler, he took his entrance examinations. When he learned the results, his sister Bamie was away on a visit. "Is it not splendid," he wrote her, "about my examinations?"

It was indeed splendid. He had passed in every subject. In September, the month before his eighteenth birthday, he left for Cambridge, and found a room in a house near Harvard Yard. Bamie went with him to help him to get settled. When she returned, the house on Fifty-seventh Street seemed very lonely without him.

It might have seemed even lonelier that winter, had it not been for Theodore's letters. He was having to study harder than he had expected, he said, but he liked Harvard. He was making new friends. His asthma still bothered him, but he felt well most of the time.

In some of his letters, there was a hint of homesickness. "I do not think there is a fellow in College," he wrote to his father, "who has a family that love him as much as you all do me. I am *sure* that there is no one who has a father who is also his best and most intimate friend, as you are mine."

When Theodore came home for Christmas, he was still thin, but his family found that he had changed into quite a young man. He had begun to take an interest in his clothes. His fair hair, in contrast to earlier days, was neatly combed. Most amazing of all, he had grown whiskers—and the whiskers were red. One day during his vacation, he and his father had a long talk.

"Father," said the son, "I want to take all the courses I can in natural history. Maybe some day I'll be a professor and teach it. I still want to be a naturalist."

This announcement was no surprise. "All right," said Mr. Roosevelt slowly, "if you are sure that is what you really want to do. But if you become a naturalist, you must be a good one. You must make it a serious career and do the best work that is in you."

"I intend to, Father."

"You would probably never earn much money, you know, and there are many pleasures you would have to do without. If you do not earn much, you must even things up by not spending much."

"I am not especially interested in making money," Theodore insisted.

Mr. Roosevelt still looked doubtful, and the same doubts began to worry Theodore after his return to college. He had so many interests, and he was constantly adding new ones. The trouble with being a professor was that he might not be able to do all of the other things he wished to do.

6

THEODORE LITTLE guessed, when he returned to Harvard, what great changes were soon to take place in his life. Both joy and sorrow lay ahead of him. The sorrow came during his sophomore year when his father died. For a while the pain in Theodore's heart seemed more than he could bear. He loved his "little Motherling" very much, but she was someone to cherish and protect; he had depended on his father for advice and understanding. "It is impossible to tell in words how terribly I miss him," he wrote in his diary. "With the help of God, I will try to live such a life as Father would have wished me to."

He must "keep up the name," he promised himself. The name Theodore Roosevelt was one to be proud of, and he must make himself worthy of it. As the weeks and months passed, he never forgot his resolve: to grow into the kind of man of whom his father would have approved.

He was doing well in his studies, and with regular exercise, his health continued to improve. He was making many friends. Not that his new friends always understood him. That fellow Roosevelt, they said, was not quite like anybody else. He kept snakes and a live turtle in his room. He skipped rope to strengthen the muscles in his legs, and he did not seem to mind if people laughed. His classmates and even his teachers sometimes thought him a little "bumptious" because he had so much to say in class.

One day, during a lecture on natural history, he raised his hand again and again. He asked question after question. Finally, the professor grew tired of being interrupted.

"Look here, Roosevelt," he said, "let me talk. I'm running this course."

The other students seemed to think this was funny, but Theodore was puzzled. He had come to college to learn; why shouldn't he ask questions? He had always been encouraged to ask questions at home.

He was glad when the time came to return home for vacation. The summer between his sophomore and junior years was spent at Tranquillity. As Theodore stood on the wide piazza between Bamie and his mother, he looked toward the blue waters of the Sound. What a lucky fellow he was! he thought. What a blessing to have such a home. With the father gone, the rest of the family had drawn closer together, as if to comfort each other.

The weeks passed quickly—weeks filled with long tramps through the woods and picnics on the shore. By August, Theodore was tanned from his days in the sun, but he could not forget his grief; he still missed his father. He decided to round out the summer by going to Island Falls in Maine with Emblen and West Roosevelt, who had been there before with his tutor, Mr. Cutler. They told him what a good place it was for fishing and hunting, and that Bill Sewall, a lumberman who also acted as a guide for hunters, was the sort of man Theodore would like.

The boys took an overnight train from Boston to a small town in northern Maine. Here they hired a horse and buckboard for the long drive to Island Falls. For thirty-six miles they traveled through deep woods, arriving at twilight at a house in the clearing. Bill Sewall, a tall, bearded man of thirty-four, came out to meet them.

"Hello, Bill!" West and Emblen greeted him warmly. "This is our cousin Theodore."

Bill Sewall glanced curiously at the slender youth who wore glasses, and put out his hand. "Mr. Cutler has told me about you," he said.

He did not add that Arthur Cutler had warned him that Theodore must not be allowed to overdo. The boy might be frail, Bill decided, but he did not look like the kind who would want to be coddled.

"I've got a different fellow to guide from what I've ever seen before," Bill told his nephew, Wilmot Dow.

Next morning, the two backwoodsmen and the three boys paddled a canoe down the river and pitched their tents on the bank for a night of camping. After that they went hunting nearly every day, and Bill found that Theodore could walk twenty-five miles and not complain. If he did not feel well, he said nothing about it. He was always fun, never "out of sorts."

"I liked him right off," said Bill later. "I liked him clear through."

The two men, the older and the younger, had much in common. Although Bill had never been to college, he had read many books. Like Theodore, he enjoyed poetry. Sometimes as they tramped together along the forest paths, he recited verse after verse. Both of them liked Longfellow's poems about the Viking hero, King Olaf. Theodore recalled two lines:

> "Meekness is weakness,
>   Strength is triumphant. . . ."

Bill Sewall smiled. "You would never know it to look at me now," he confided, "but *I* used to be a sickly boy."

"You?" said Theodore in surprise.

"Yes, but hard work cured me," Bill replied. "When I was sixteen my father was taken ill, and I had to take my ax and start cutting down trees to help support the family."

Neither spoke for a few minutes. Then Bill added softly, "They tell us that prayer is the desire of the heart, and I desired above all else to be well and strong."

Theodore glanced at his new friend admiringly. Bill Sewall, like his father, was a man to look up to.

He liked Bill's friends, too. Once they spent several days in a lumber camp, and it did not seem to matter that most of the crew could not even write their names. These men had spent their lives in the backwoods, and the stories they told around their campfire were true. They reminded Theodore of the pioneers in his favorite books.

"I've read about such things," he told Bill afterwards, "but those fellows know what they're talking about."

The lumbermen felt much the same way about him. "Why, he's as plain as a spruce board," said one man, "and as square as a brick."

That first visit to Island Falls lasted eighteen days, and Theodore promised to return in the spring. On the train that took him back to college, he was thinking how much he had enjoyed roughing it. His life at Harvard, as a popular member of the junior class, would be different. He would enjoy that, too. He always looked forward to whatever new adventures might be waiting.

His next adventure was to fall in love. A few weeks after his return to Cambridge, he met Alice Lee. Alice, the cousin of his friend Richard Saltonstall, lived in Chestnut Hill, near Boston. She and her sister Rose played tennis with Theodore and Richard. The four took long hikes and went dancing. Rose was amused, because Theodore's movements were so awkward and jerky.

"Why, he doesn't dance," she said to herself. "He hops."

Theodore was not worried about the way he looked. He was thinking only of the pretty younger sister with the laughing gray eyes who seemed to float in his arms to the music of the waltz. By Thanksgiving he knew that he wanted Alice to be his wife.

"See that girl," he said to a friend one day, "I am going to marry her. She won't have me, but I am going to have *her*."

Alice was only seventeen, and he was afraid that her parents would consider her too young to marry. The following June he finally screwed up his courage to ask her. He kept on asking her, off and on, for the next eight months. One evening in January of his senior year, he decided that he could not bear the suspense any longer. He hitched up Lightfoot and drove to Chestnut Hill. When he returned he felt much calmer.

"At last everything is settled," he wrote in his diary. "I am so happy that I dare not trust in my own happiness. My own sweet, pretty darling consented to be my wife . . . The aim of my whole life shall be to make her happy."

For several months Theodore had been trying to decide what work he should do after he finished college. He was still interested in nature, but he wanted to observe it at first hand; to wander through the countryside gathering specimens. His professors of natural history, he had discovered, spent most of their time peering into their microscopes, and he thought that a very dull way to study nature. Would such a quiet life ever satisfy him?

Perhaps he should be a writer. He liked to write, and during his senior year he began a book, *The Naval War of 1812*. He also enjoyed his classes in political science, and he became interested in government. One day he had a talk with one of his professors. Should he spend more time on political science, or should he go ahead with his studies in natural history?

"Political science is the field where I feel more work is most needed," the professor said.

As always, when trying to make a decision, Theodore wondered what his father would have advised. Although Theodore Roosevelt, Sr. had not been a politician, he had always been interested in public welfare. He had tried to help others, and his son wanted to follow his example. Toward the end of his senior year, he decided to study law. Later, perhaps, he told a friend, he could go into public life.

The two young men were seated on a windowseat that looked out over Harvard Yard. The old brick buildings, ivy-covered, were only shadowy outlines in the soft spring night. "I am going to try to help the cause of better government in New York City," said Theodore. Then he added uncertainly, "I don't know exactly how."

The past four years had been very happy ones. He had come to college a shy, sickly boy. Now he was much stronger. He had had fun. His grades had been excellent, and in June he would graduate with honors.

"No man ever had so pleasant a college course," he wrote in his diary. "Above everything else put together, I have won the sweetest of girls for my wife."

7

THE WEDDING took place on October 27, 1880—Theodore Roosevelt's twenty-second birthday—and he and his bride spent their honeymoon at Tranquillity. "I can never express how much I love her," he wrote in his diary.

The next winter was a busy one. The money Theodore had inherited from his father made it possible for him to attend Columbia Law School and to continue work on his book. But he was restless, and he had not forgotten his resolve to help the cause of better government. How could one get started in politics? he asked some of his older friends. Was there a political club that he could join?

His friends were shocked. They told him that most of the politicians who managed the state and city governments were dishonest.

Certainly a young man of good family would not want to join a political club. He would meet only saloonkeepers and people like that.

Theodore threw back his head. His blue eyes flashed behind the thick-lensed spectacles. "You mean the people I know do *not* belong to the governing class, and that those other people do?" he asked sharply. "Well, I intend to belong to the governing class, also."

He thought it was wrong to criticize dishonest government and then not try to do anything to make it better. When he learned of a Republican Club in his own part of the city, he asked to join it. After a few meetings, he declared that he was having a "bully time." The fact that the men he met were different from the people he had always known only made them seem more interesting.

The other members of the club were not quite so sure about Theodore—not at first. His fine clothes, his side whiskers, and the eyeglasses, which he wore at the end of a black silk ribbon, made him look rather elegant. They called him "a dude," but they could not help liking him. When he became a candidate for the Assembly, he was elected. His new friends, and many of his old ones from the richest section of the city, had turned out to vote for him.

The Assembly was a part of the State Legislature that made the laws for the State of New York. Theodore Roosevelt was only twenty-three years old when he arrived in Albany, the capital, to begin his new work in January 1882. He was the youngest member of the Assembly, probably the richest member, and—in the words of one newspaper reporter—"as green as grass." He had "a good honest laugh," and "his teeth seemed to be all over his face." The older men were amused by his Harvard accent, and they thought that his first name was "sissy." They soon found out, however, that he was anything but a sissy. He was smart. He was very much in earnest. And he had courage.

His courage was soon to be tested. Some of the newspaper writers had accused a well-known judge of being dishonest. They said he had helped certain big business men who had cheated the public out of large sums of money. Theodore was indignant. Within a few weeks after he had entered the Assembly, he arose behind his desk to make a speech. He asked that the members appoint a committee to find out the truth. The people of the state, he said, had a right to demand that a judge be honest. If this one *was* honest, he should have a chance to prove it.

The leaders in both political parties—the "bosses," as they were called—were angry and frightened. They had a great deal of influence in the Assembly, and they said that "the young man from New York" should be careful what he said about a well-known and respected judge. Theodore suspected that they were trying to hush up the scandal because they, too, were dishonest. Their chief interest was in making as much money as they could for themselves, and they did not seem to care if the people of the state *were* cheated.

Even the honest members of the Assembly were worried, and Theodore was warned not to make the bosses too angry. "Just sit on your coattails for a while," his friends advised him. He knew, if the bosses were against him, he might never be elected again, but he would not listen. The next week he made another speech.

It did no good. The Assembly still refused to consider his suggestion, but some of the newspaper writers began to take his part. They admired his courage.

"Mr. Roosevelt," said one writer, "has a most refreshing habit of calling men and things by their right names."

And then the newspaper readers became interested. For the first time, many of them realized how certain "political bullies" were cheating the people. They wrote angry letters to their representatives in the Assembly, demanding that Roosevelt's suggestion be voted on again.

This time when the votes were counted, it was found that only six men still held out against him. One hundred and four members voted for the investigation that he wanted.

Suddenly he found himself famous. Because he had dared to fight for what he thought was right, his name had become known throughout the state. The voters in his own district elected him to a second—and then to a third—term in the Assembly.

During the summer of his second term, Theodore was ill again with asthma. Alice was expecting a baby the following February, and she decided to stay on with his mother, while he took a vacation in the Dakotas. He hoped that the dry, clear air would make it easier to breathe.

Also he wanted to see the "Wild West," of which he had read. The West, where Indians had galloped over the plains after herds of thundering buffalo, would not be "wild" much longer. The Indians had been driven out, and cattle were beginning to take the place of buffalo on the vast grasslands. Theodore—who was still a boy at heart and always would be—wanted to go on a buffalo hunt before it was too late.

When he arrived early one September morning at the last town on the railroad, he found only a few scattered buildings. At first, no one seemed interested in hunting buffalo. Then he met Joe Ferris. Joe informed him that the only buffalo left in the entire region were about forty or fifty miles up the river.

"Will you take me there?" asked Theodore eagerly. "Will you be my guide on a buffalo hunt?"

Joe was about to say "No." At first glance he had sized up Theodore as a "tenderfoot"—a man not used to the hardships of the West. He was pale and skinny, certainly not strong enough to go hunting. And then Joe took a second look. There was something about the firm set of the tenderfoot's jaw that he liked.

"When do you want to start?" he asked.

"The sooner the better," Theodore replied.

"All right. I'll get the horses ready. Gregor Lang has a cow camp up that way. He'll let us stop with him."

When the two men arrived at the camp—Joe riding in a buckboard with the supplies and Theodore following on horseback—they were cordially welcomed. Gregor offered Theodore his bunk, but the young man from the East refused. He rolled up in a blanket on the dirt floor and slept soundly all night. The next morning it was raining, and Joe suggested that they wait until the weather cleared.

"Why wait?" asked Theodore.

Joe was not going to "lie down" to any tenderfoot, and he reluctantly mounted his horse. All that day they rode over slushy ground. The next morning they went again—and the next morning after that. Then for several nights they camped out. On the fifth day they came upon buffalo tracks, and after a long, dreary ride they saw three big shaggy beasts.

It was twilight when they cautiously approached. Theodore raised his gun. At that moment his horse reared, and he succeeded only in wounding one of the buffalo. All three lumbered off into the darkness.

The hunters returned to camp but continued to hunt in the daytime. Bad luck seemed to follow them. Once a wolf caused their exhausted horses to stampede. Theodore was thrown over his horse's head, and another time it sank up to its withers in a soft mud hole. Theodore tied a rope around it, and scrambled to the bank. With the help of Joe and Joe's horse, he finally managed to pull his own frightened horse to safety.

At the end of two weeks they spotted another buffalo. The wind was blowing toward them. The big animal was not aware that they had dismounted and were creeping closer. Theodore raised his gun and fired.

"I've got him! I've got him!" he yelled.

He jumped around like an Indian in a war dance, while Joe looked on wearily. He was "plumb tired out," but his frail-looking companion, now covered with mud from head to foot, was really enjoying himself.

48

"That tenderfoot sure can stand a lot of hard knocks," said Joe to himself. "You just can't knock him out of sorts."

Each evening after their return to camp, Joe would roll up in his blanket and soon be sound asleep. Theodore would sit up with Gregor Lang until past midnight. As he gazed into the fire, he thought how much he liked this wild country. He liked the stark, lonely beauty of the rolling plains and deep ragged gulches. He had noticed the thick grass that grew in the bottom lands near the rivers. He had seen cattle—hundreds of them—grazing there, and Gregor was convinced that a fortune could be made in the cattle business. Theodore decided to invest some of the money that his father had left him.

"If I bought a herd, would you manage it for me?" he asked one night.

"I wish I could," Gregor replied, "but I am already tied up with another man and he is counting on me. Why don't you ask Joe's brother, Sylvane Ferris, and his partner, William Merrifield? They are now managing an outfit farther up the river near Chimney Butte. They are good square fellows and they'll do right by you."

Theodore remembered Chimney Butte, the tall butte or mountain whose steep clay slopes had a sort of grandeur very different from the gentle hills of the East. He and Joe had stopped for a brief visit with Sylvane and William in the crude log buildings which they called their "ranch." They owned the buildings, but the land—like the vast acres known as "the range"—was public land. Most of it belonged to the United States Government, and cattle were allowed to graze freely there. The herds of cattle that Theodore had seen at Chimney Butte belonged to two men in St. Paul. Sylvane Ferris and William Merrifield were managing the herds for a share of the profits.

"Maybe the St. Paul men will be willing to sell out to you," Gregor suggested. "Anyway, I'll send for Sylvane and William, and you can talk it over with them."

Everything happened very quickly after that. The two young

49

men rode down to Gregor's camp, looking very picturesque in their sombreros, the wide-brimmed hats cowboys wore. They were interested in working for Mr. Roosevelt, and they believed that their present employers would be willing to sell. Theodore gave them a check and they left for St. Paul.

Theodore continued to hunt, but the next few days were anxious ones. Then came a telegram from William Merrifield. He had purchased the Chimney Butte outfit in Theodore's name, and Theodore was in the cattle business. He was bubbling over with enthusiasm when he boarded the train for New York.

He felt better than he had for months. He would go back to Dakota every year for a vacation, he decided. Perhaps next summer Alice could come with him. He could hardly wait to see her.

Never had a couple seemed happier. Theodore had bought not only a ranch in Dakota but also land in Oyster Bay, and he was going to build a house for Alice on his favorite hill. Night after night, during that fall and winter, they pored over the plans the architect had drawn, and talked about their new home. Each Sunday evening Theodore had to leave for Albany where the Assembly was meeting. All week he looked forward to Friday when he could return to his young wife.

"Back again . . . with my own sunny darling," read one entry in his diary. "I can imagine nothing more happy in life than an evening in my own cozy little sitting room."

Theodore was in Albany when the telegram came that he had a little daughter, and he took the first train home. The cab drew up before the door of his mother's house, where Alice was staying, and he rushed up the steps. It was one of the most anxious, yet one of the happiest, moments of his life.

The door opened. He knew at once that something was wrong, terribly wrong. Elliott stood there, pale and shaken. "There is a curse on this house," Elliott told him. "Mother is dying, and Alice is dying, too."

Within a few hours the two people whom Theodore loved best in the world were gone. He was numb with grief. He hardly seemed to know what he was doing. His sister Bamie was caring for the new baby, named Alice Lee for her mother. And Theodore went back to the Assembly. Only work, he decided, could help him to bear his sorrow.

"It was a grim and evil fate," he wrote in answer to a letter from Bill Sewall. "But I have never believed it did any good to flinch or yield for any blow, nor does it lighten the blow to cease from working."

He did not want anyone to sympathize with him—his grief was too deep. He did not want to talk about it, but there was a sadness in his face that his family and friends had never seen before. He had a busy spring in the Assembly. He also was busy in New York, for he went ahead with plans for building a house at Oyster Bay. Baby Alice Lee must have a home, and he wanted her to grow up among his friends and cousins.

In June he went West again. He planned to come back often to see his "darling baby" but he was through with politics—or so he thought. He was going to live on his ranch. He was going to work as hard as any cowboy.

Before he began his new life, he put together a little book to give to the friends of the girl that he had loved.

"She was beautiful in face and form," he wrote on the first page, "and lovelier still in spirit; as a flower she grew and as a fair young flower she died . . . And when my heart's dearest died, the light went out of my life forever."

Love—a great love—was to come to Theodore again. But Alice Lee was to remain a sweet and tender memory locked forever in his heart.

8

THEODORE'S SPIRITS rose when he rode out over the range with Sylvane Ferris and William Merrifield. The animals he saw grazing there belonged to a number of different outfits, but each one bore the brand, or mark, of its owner. The brand of the Chimney Butte ranch was in the shape of a Maltese cross, and the new owner felt much encouraged when he saw his sleek, healthy-looking cows.

"I regard the outlook for making the business a success as very hopeful," he wrote Bamie. "I shall put in a thousand more cattle and make it my regular business. The country is growing on me more and more; it has a curious, fantastic beauty of its own."

His idea was to start a second ranch and put his friends, Bill Sewall and Bill's nephew, Wilmot Dow, in charge. He had written them earlier, but before he asked them to come so far, he had wanted to see for himself how his cattle had gotten through the winter. Now he decided to go ahead with his plan, and Sylvane and William left for Minnesota to buy a small herd for the new ranch. Then Theodore mounted his horse and went on a hunting trip.

He went alone—something he had wanted to do ever since he was a boy! He wanted to prove that he could manage by himself. One day he would canter mile after mile over smooth, green grass, with roses blooming in the thickets. The next morning would find him in a wild region of winding canyons and strange-shaped buttes. At night he wrapped himself in a blanket and lay on the ground under a canopy of stars.

He felt very free—and very lonely. He did not expect to be happy ever again, but in this wild country that he had learned to love, he might find his sorrow easier to bear.

Back at Chimney Butte, Theodore found that Sylvane and William had not returned. George Myer, a cowboy who had recently joined the outfit, was looking after the cattle and horses.

"I'm also the cook," said George. "Anything special you'd like for supper?"

Theodore's mouth watered. Yes, there was something, he decided, after several days of doing his own cooking over a campfire. "Some baking powder biscuits would taste good," he suggested.

"Sure thing," George replied. "Where's the baking powder?" He reached for a can on the shelf above the stove and started to mix the dough. He rolled it out and cut the biscuits. They looked white and delicious when he popped them into the oven. Theodore was becoming hungrier by the minute, as George set out tin plates and tin knives and forks on the rough board table. On each plate there was a slice of venison, but Theodore was waiting for the biscuits.

"Here they come," said George proudly, and reached for the pan. "Well, what do you know!"

The biscuits were a bright emerald green!

"What do you know!" George repeated. "There must have been soda in that can. I thought it was baking powder."

Theodore was disappointed, but thought it was a good joke. "Tomorrow," he announced firmly, "*I* shall do the cooking."

The next morning while George was busy with chores outdoors, Theodore started a fire in the stove, found a kettle, poured in some rice, and added water. He sat down to write a letter, but after a few minutes he smelled something burning. The rice had begun to swell and was spilling over on the stove. He pulled every dish off the shelf and filled it with half-cooked rice. He filled every pot and every pan. He filled the water pitcher. He filled the wash basin.

A shadow darkened the doorway, and he realized that he was being watched. "Do you like to cook, Mr. Roosevelt?" asked George.

Both men were laughing. "All right," Theodore replied. "I turn the cooking back to you. But no more green biscuits, please."

The next day Theodore started on another trip. Some forty miles down the river, he came upon just the place he wanted for a second ranch. On the ground he noticed the interlocked horns of two elk that had died fighting, and he named his new ranch the Elkhorn. Then he took the train for New York, where Bill Sewall and Wilmot Dow joined him. He warned them that if they went West with him they could not expect to make a fortune the first year or two, but he would give them a share of whatever profits there were.

"If I lose money instead," he said, "I guarantee to pay you wages. Whatever happens, you shall not lose by it."

"That's a pretty one-sided agreement," said Bill, "but if you can stand it, I guess we can."

It was the first time Bill and Wilmot had ever been West, and they were amazed by the panorama of jagged mountains and seemingly endless plains unfolding outside the train windows. There were vast stretches of grass—sometimes an acre, sometimes a hundred acres— and then other stretches of barren landscape where no green thing grew. They got off the train at the little town of Medora and rode out to Chimney Butte.

"Well, what do you think of the country?" asked Theodore.

Bill did not answer at once. "I like the country well enough," he said finally. "But I don't believe it is much of a cattle country."

"Everybody out here says it is. You don't know anything about it, Bill."

"It's a fact, I don't know much about it," Bill admitted. "But that's the way it looks to me, like not much of a cattle country."

The cattle that Sylvane and William had purchased in Minnesota had arrived, and the next morning Bill and Wilmot set out for Elkhorn ranch, driving the herd before them. For several months after that they were busy learning the cattle business. They lived in a small shack near the river while they cut down trees and built a log house. By spring it was ready and Theodore moved in with his friends.

"I do not see how anyone could have lived more comfortably," he said later. "I got out a rocking chair—I am fond of rocking chairs— and enough books to fill two or three shelves, and a rubber bathtub so that I could get a bath. We had buffalo robes and bearskins of our own killing. There were at least two rooms that were always warm, even in the bitterest weather, and we had plenty to eat."

He frequently rode back and forth the forty miles between his two ranches, and he went on long hunting trips. His first book about the War of 1812, published two years earlier, had been a success, and now he was writing another one, *Hunting Trips of a Ranchman*. He tried to keep busy every minute, but there were times when he could not help feeling discouraged.

"I have nothing left to live for," he told Bill one day. "What difference does it make what becomes of me?"

"I feel like going for you bowlegged when you talk like that," said Bill. "You have your child to live for."

"Her aunt can take better care of her than I can," Theodore replied. "She would be just as well off without me."

"You won't always feel that way," Bill went on in a kinder tone. "I have had troubles, too, but time heals them over. You won't always be willing to stay here. Some day you will want to get back among your friends where you can be more benefit to the world than you can here driving cattle."

There was no answer, and Bill tried again. "You can go home and start a reform, can't you? You always want to make things better instead of worse. You would make a good reformer."

Theodore shrugged his shoulders; he thought that he was through with politics. But that was the last time he spoke of having nothing to live for. Perhaps he decided that he was not being a good sport about his troubles, and he resolved to show more courage.

Ever since Theodore could remember he had tried to be courageous. Since coming to Dakota, he had proved his courage as a hunter, but he knew that he was still considered a tenderfoot. The cowboys called him "Four-eyes" because of his glasses, but he paid no attention. There was always plenty of work to be done on a ranch, and he simply went ahead and did his share of the chores.

One morning he rode off in search of several horses that had wandered away, and night found him thirty miles from home. There were no houses close by, except in the little settlement of Mingusville. As he dismounted before the small, shabby hotel, two shots rang out from inside. Theodore hesitated. Law-abiding ranchmen still lived in fear of cattle thieves and other "bad men," and he wanted to avoid trouble. But the night was cold and he was hungry. He stabled his horse and went inside.

The room was crowded with sheepherders, and they looked scared. All eyes were on a rough-looking man in a wide-brimmed hat standing at the bar. He held a gun in each hand, and was yelling at the top of his lungs.

He glanced toward the door. "Here comes Four-eyes," he said, sneering. "Four-eyes is going to treat everyone to drinks."

The sheepherders laughed nervously. Theodore walked over to

the stove and sat down, hoping that the drunken bully would soon forget him. Instead, the man followed him, brandishing both guns. He came so close that Theodore could feel his hot breath.

"Didn't you hear me?" he shouted. "I said Four-eyes was going to treat."

Theodore Roosevelt looked around the room. Everyone was watching. He glanced down at the bully's feet. Why, the man was a fool! With feet so close together, he could easily be knocked off balance. He was yelling again. He seemed to explode in a volley of swear words that Theodore had never even heard before. One thing was certain—the fellow wanted him to treat!

Theodore stood up. "If I've got to, I suppose I've got to," he said.

At that instant his right hand shot out. The bully felt a sharp blow on his jaw. Before he quite knew what was happening, another blow came from Theodore's left. The two guns went off, but the shots went wide. The bully fell, knocking his head against the side of the bar. The fall knocked him unconscious and the sheepherders, suddenly grown very brave, hurried him outside into a shed.

The story of how the tenderfoot had won a fight with a bully, of whom everyone else was afraid, soon reached Medora. The ranchmen and their cowboys no longer called Theodore "Four-eyes" but "Old Four-eyes." It was now a nickname that showed how much they liked and admired him.

They still "joshed" him now and then, but he did not mind. He took a small boy's pride in his cowboy outfit. "You would be amused," he wrote to a friend back East, "to see me in my broad sombrero hat, buckskin shirt, horsehair riding trousers, and boots and silver spurs."

His way of speaking caused much amusement. His high voice and clipped accent sounded very different from the lazy drawl of the cowboys. He never used swear words, the way most of them did. To hear him exclaim, "By Godfrey!" sounded strange to the cowboys, but many of their slang words sounded just as strange to him.

He soon learned that a bronco, or "bronc," was a Westerner's name for a small, spirited horse. A "maverick" usually meant a calf that did not bear the brand of any owner. "Chow" meant food. It was served from a "chuck wagon" during a "roundup."

The roundup was the hardest and the most interesting part of a ranchman's life. There were few fences at that time, and the cattle wandered many miles in search of good grazing grass. Every spring the ranchmen and their cowboys rode out together over the range to round up and sort out their own cattle and to find the new little calves born during the winter. Usually a calf followed its mother, and the mother bore the brand of the ranch to which she belonged. After a calf was caught it was dragged to the fire where the owner's brand was put on its skin with a hot iron. Although the hurt was soon over, the calf set up a loud bawling and tried to get away.

Theodore, according to William Merrifield, "could wrastle a calf as good as anybody." There was no task too hard for him. After a night wrapped in his blanket on the ground, he got up at three o'clock in the morning when the call for breakfast came. Many days he spent fourteen or sixteen hours in the saddle. Sometimes, in stormy weather, he went twenty-four hours without sleep.

"That four-eyed maverick has got sand in his craw aplenty," said one of his new friends.

Roundups were not all hardship. After evening chow the cowboys often told tall tales or sang cowboy songs around the campfire. The faces of the men, ruddy in the firelight, had lost their weariness. They had forgotten the hard work of the day, but for some of them the work was not over. Each had to take a turn at night watch.

Two night guards usually worked together in two-hour stretches. Around and around the herd they rode, always watchful for the least sign of restlessness. A coyote howling in the distance, a sudden clap of thunder, a white flash of lightning, might frighten the cattle into a stampede, and it soothed them to hear the cowboys sing. One night as Theodore made his rounds, he was humming a song:

"The days that I was hard up,
I never shall forget.
The days that I was hard up—
I may be well off yet. . . ."

The lines might have been meant just for him. He had never been "hard up" in the way that the song meant, but he had known great sorrow. Time had helped to heal his grief, as Bill had told him it would—time and hard work. Under the stars, he felt at peace.

He had another reason to be grateful. He had never felt better. The rugged weeks in the open had accomplished what Theodore Roosevelt had been striving for since he was a boy. His asthma seldom bothered him. He no longer coughed and wheezed, trying to get his breath. The thin shoulders had broadened. His chest had widened. Even his neck seemed bigger. He looked like a real Westerner.

The roundup was over in June, and Theodore left for New York to arrange for the publication of his book. When his train stopped in St. Paul, newspaper reporters who had interviewed him before came to see him. How he had changed! they thought. It was hard to realize that this was the pale, thin young man who had gone West only a year earlier. His face was deeply tanned from days in the sun, and he had gained thirty pounds in weight.

Theodore was still wearing a woolen shirt, with a big handkerchief tied loosely around his neck in true Western style. "Yes, I am a regular cowboy," he boasted. "There is more excitement in the roundup than in politics. Honestly, I would not go back to New York if I had no interests there. I prefer my ranch, and the excitement it brings, to New York life, though I always make it a point to enjoy myself wherever I am."

9

THE BIG rambling house on the hill overlooking Long Island Sound was finished. This was the same hill where, as a boy, Theodore had hunted specimens and gone on picnics.

It was here that old Chief Sagamore Mohannis had held war councils in the days when Indians roamed the island. Sagamore Hill— that should be the name of his new home, Theodore decided. Bamie would live there during the summer with little Alice Lee Roosevelt. It would be an ideal place for his baby to grow up.

Baby Lee, as her father called her, was sixteen months old that June of 1885, and already she was showing a sturdy independence and lively curiosity so like his own. His eyes softened as he watched her toddle toward him across the wide veranda, and he swept her up into his arms. Each time they were together, he found it harder to leave.

But he was needed on his ranch, and here he found another small girl, Kitty Sewall, waiting to welcome him. During Theodore's absence, the wives of Bill and Wilmot had arrived in Dakota, and the two women made the log house seem more homelike. There were now curtains at the windows, and Mrs. Sewall's cooking was much better than her husband's.

"We were all a very happy family at Elkhorn Ranch," said Bill. "When we were through with the day's work, Theodore would sit before the fire and tell stories of his hunting trips, or about history that he had read. He was the best-read man I ever saw."

Theodore not only had read a great deal of history; he was helping to make history even then. The Mingusville bully was one of many "bad men" who had come into the Western cattle country. Thieves robbed honest ranchmen of horses and cattle, and spread terror wherever they went. Even the sheriffs were afraid of them. Occasionally, a bad man would be arrested, but there was no law court closer than the town of Dickinson forty miles away. In a day of hard travel it was small wonder that many criminals never even went to trial.

A few months after Theodore went West to live, he had called a meeting of neighboring ranchmen. By working together, they hoped to prevent thieves from stealing their cattle and, in time, to bring law and order to the region. The ranchmen had elected him their president, and in the fall of 1885, he was made a deputy sheriff of his county. The young man of twenty-seven, who only a year before had been laughed at as a tenderfoot, was becoming known throughout Dakota territory. One newspaper editor, who was looking forward to the time when Dakota would become a state, suggested that he should be a candidate for Congress.

Theodore shook his head. Perhaps he was beginning to realize that Bill Sewall was right. Much as he liked the West, he might not want to stay there always. Although he hardly realized it himself, he was lonely and homesick, and letters from his family were eagerly read. He continued to make frequent trips to New York, and one day in the fall of 1885 he met Edith Carow again. "Her Ladyship" was still calm and dignified—and very lovely.

They saw a great deal of each other that winter, and Theodore realized that he need not be lonely any longer. They became secretly engaged, but they could not be married at once. Edith was to join her family in London. Theodore had to return to Dakota. The months before he would see her again seemed like years, but he had no time to mope. He was writing another book, and he looked forward to helping in the big general roundup that spring.

When he arrived at Elkhorn Ranch, he found Bill Sewall feeling very discouraged. Bill was afraid there was not enough grass to feed so many cattle, yet more and more were being brought in every year. Theodore, thinking ahead to a happy life with Edith, refused to worry. He went hunting for a few hours nearly every day, but with the cold north winds blowing, it was a good time for staying indoors. He spent most of his time writing.

Then one morning Bill discovered that their only boat had been stolen during the night. The rope had been cut, and one of the thieves had dropped a glove on the shore. The closest neighbor lived fifteen miles away, but Mike Finnegan had been staying in a shack just around the bend in the river. Mike was known to be a thief. He had stolen so many horses and cattle that some of the ranchmen had been threatening to hang him. Bill strode into the cabin as Theodore was finishing his breakfast.

"It's that ornery Mike Finnegan," said Bill, "and those two friends who have been holing up with him in the shack. Most likely they decided it was healthier for them to get out of the country."

Theodore jumped to his feet. "And with our only boat?" he shouted. "Let's not waste time. We'll have to go after them."

Bill had never seen Theodore so angry—and not only because of the loss of the boat. As deputy sheriff, his duty was to see that the laws were obeyed. Mike had been defying those laws long enough, often at the point of a gun. To let him go unpunished would encourage him, and others like him, to commit more crimes.

"We'll have to go after them," Theodore said again. "Let's get the horses saddled."

"The ground's too slippery for the horses," Bill objected, "and we'd never get near the river on horseback. There is too much snow piled up along the banks. Wilmot and I will have to build another boat."

The boat was ready in four days, but it was scarcely finished when a blizzard struck. The wind blew so fiercely that even the timbers of the cabin shook, and another three days passed before the men dared to venture outdoors. When they finally started, the temperature had dropped to below zero. The water was filled with huge cakes of floating ice, and ice formed on the long poles they used to guide the

boat. Their hands were stiff with cold, and the north wind was in their faces.

At night they camped on shore, shivering under their furs and blankets. Morning would find them floating down the stream again. Theodore, who seldom went anywhere without a book, spent part of his time reading, and at times he almost forgot how cold he was. By the third afternoon the three men had traveled more than a hundred miles. Rounding a bend in the river, they saw a thin line of smoke from a campfire.

"There's our boat!" said Bill.

Theodore looked more closely. The stolen boat had been dragged up on the bank. Was Mike Finnegan or one of his companions hiding behind those cottonwood bushes? He knew that they would not hesitate to shoot.

"Better have your guns ready," Bill added in a low voice.

Theodore and Wilmot already had their pistols buckled on. Each grabbed a rifle and jumped for the shore. The current was swift, and Bill lagged behind to tie up the new boat. In the distance, he could hear someone shouting, "Put up your hands." He rushed toward the campfire, his rifle ready, fearing that Theodore and Wilmot were in danger.

They had been in danger, of course, but Theodore made light of it when he wrote to Bamie a few days later. "We came upon their camp by surprise," he told her, "and, covering them with our cocked rifles, 'held them up' and disarmed them in the most approved Western fashion."

The capture of Mike Finnegan and his companions was not so easy as Theodore made it sound. It was even harder to decide what to do with them. The nearest jail was miles away in Dickinson. The prisoners were marched to the boats, but they had to be watched every minute to prevent their escape. They could not be tied, for fear that their hands and feet might freeze. A few miles downstream the boats ran into an ice jam and were nearly sucked under. There was nothing to do but to return to camp. The supply of food was running low, and everyone was hungry.

Finally the ice in the river broke up enough for captors and prisoners to continue their journey. When they finally reached a cowcamp on the shore, Theodore borrowed a horse and rode inland to a ranch. Here he hired a team and wagon. It would be quicker, he suggested, for him to take the prisoners overland to Dickinson. Bill and Wilmot would continue down the river with the boats.

The overland trip was probably the hardest part of the journey. Theodore walked behind the wagon, his gun still cocked. His fringed buckskin jacket was in rags, his chaps covered with mud. He was hungry and cold. His feet were blistered. But he plodded on, mile after dreary mile, until he reached Dickinson. With a sigh of relief, he turned the prisoners over to the sheriff.

Thirteen days had passed since he set out from the Elkhorn Ranch. Every bone in his body seemed to ache. He was limping down the street when he saw a man approaching.

"Good afternoon," said Theodore, "can you direct me to a doctor?"

"I'm Dr. Stickney," was the reply. "I am the only doctor in this whole surrounding country."

"By George," said Theodore, and he seemed to bite off the words. "You're exactly the man I want to see. I've just come forty miles on foot, bringing some horse thieves, and my feet are so badly blistered I can hardly walk."

A few minutes later the doctor was bandaging the blistered feet. He listened in amazement to Theodore's story.

"Do you know, Mister," he asked, "what most men out here would have done? They'd have hanged those thieves out of hand. The ornery critters would have killed *you* if they had had the chance."

Theodore looked surprised. "I didn't come out here to kill anyone," he said. "All that I wanted was to defend myself and my property. There wasn't anyone to defend them for me, so I had to do it myself."

The Fourth of July that same year of 1886 Theodore returned to Dickinson to make a speech. He reminded his audience that they were opening up a new land, and because they were among the first to live there they could do more to shape its history than those who came after them. "It is not what we have that will make us a great nation," he said; "it is the way we use it." The speech made a big hit. Joe Ferris, who had been Theodore's first friend in Dakota, was especially impressed.

"What do you know!" said one of the cowboys to another. "That fool Joe Ferris says that Roosevelt is going to be President some day."

Some of the cowboys and ranchmen laughed. Others did not laugh, including Bill Sewall. He expected great things of Theodore Roosevelt.

He was not so enthusiastic about Theodore's ranch. That fall when Wilmot Dow took the cattle to market in Chicago, he had to sell for less than it had cost to raise them.

"Wilmot and I have been thinking things over," Bill told Theodore in September. "I think we'd better quit the cattle business and go back home. Fact is, the quicker we get out of here, the less money you're going to lose. I never had any money of my own to fool away, and I don't want to fool away anybody else's money either."

Theodore was disappointed. Bill was right when he said that too many cattle were being brought into Dakota to graze on the range. All the same Theodore felt confident that there would be enough grass— if only the coming winter was not too severe. He was willing to take the risk, but he realized that his friends could not afford to. He also knew that their wives were homesick for Maine.

The next few days passed in a flurry of packing. Theodore also was getting ready to leave. A short time before he had received a letter from New York with a surprising piece of news. Some of his friends were urging him to be a candidate for mayor of the city in the fall election. He wasn't at all sure that this was what he wanted. If he returned to New York to live, he would miss the stark beauty of Dakota. Yet he could not ask Edith to share the hardships of ranch life, and nothing was more important to him than their happiness together. He was sailing in December for London, where they would be married.

The day before Theodore left for New York, he and Bill had a long talk. "I've been trying to decide what I should do," said Theodore. "I don't know whether to study law again, or go into politics."

"You'd make a good lawyer," Bill replied, "but if you want my advice I'd say go into politics. Good men like you are needed. Besides, if you do go into politics, your chance to be President is good."

Theodore was embarrassed. "Now, Bill," he said, "you're looking a long way ahead. You have more faith in me than I have in myself."

The next day he pressed his face against the window of the train for a last look at the jagged buttes. William Merrifield had agreed to look after both ranches, but Theodore knew by now that the cattle business would never make him a fortune. What he *had* gained was more important. In Dakota he had found health. He had learned to know people, not just the well-to-do families of his boyhood, but plain people who worked with their hands. They were pioneers who, like the earlier settlers along the Atlantic coast, were forging a nation out of the wilderness. His two years in this wild, beautiful country had been a great adventure.

And now a different kind of adventure lay ahead. He was to run for mayor in the city where he had been born. It was an exciting prospect. But whether he won or lost, whether his cattle business improved or not, the future looked bright.

For, in London, Edith was waiting.

10

THEODORE ROOSEVELT ran for mayor—and lost. "Anyway, I had a bully time," he said. In December 1886, he sailed for London where he and Edith were married. Then they left for Italy to spend their honeymoon.

"You have no idea how sweet Edith is," Theodore wrote his sister Corinne. "I don't think even I had known how wonderfully *good* and unselfish she was."

While in Italy he received distressing news about his ranch. Dakota had had its worst winter in many years. Blizzards swept over the barren ranges, and people in lonely cabins froze to death. Thousands upon thousands of cattle had died. That spring after Theodore and his bride returned to the United States, he went West, and found conditions even worse than he had expected. Everywhere he saw dead animals lying on the ground. The starving cattle had eaten every blade of grass that they could root out from underneath the snow.

He was grateful that his friends had been spared during the cruel winter, but he himself had lost a great deal of money. He hoped that he would not have to sell Sagamore Hill.

Back home he settled down to write in the big room on the third floor. The windows on one side looked out over peaceful fields and woods. To the north could be seen the blue waters of Long Island Sound. But Theodore's thoughts went back, often and more often, to the jagged buttes of Dakota. Few people in the East had ever seen them. Nor had they seen the vast prairies where tall green grasses, ruffled by the wind, stretched away toward the horizon. He wanted to tell these people about the explorers and pioneers who, pushing westward, had settled a continent. He wanted to write a book, perhaps several books, about *The Winning of the West*.

Although worried about money, Theodore was very happy with Edith and three-year-old Alice. In October 1887, Theodore, Jr. was born. They called him Ted. Two years later came a golden-haired brother whom they named Kermit. As soon as they were old enough, their father delighted in playing "bear" with them, and his fierce growls made them shriek with laughter. Sometimes he pretended to be a horse, or rode them "piggyback" up and down the stairs. He always had a new story to tell, and he liked to tell stories as much as the children liked to hear them.

He also liked to write books, but he wanted to *do* things as well as write about them. In 1889 he accepted a position as Civil Service Commissioner in the Federal Government, and for the next six years the family lived in Washington. His new work kept him very busy during the day, but he continued to write in his spare time, usually after the children were in bed. On Sunday afternoon he took them for a "scramble" in the wild and beautiful woodland known as Rock Creek Park. Kermit was just a baby, but there were no rocks so rough or cliffs so tall that Alice and Ted did not try to scramble over them.

"I take the utmost enjoyment out of my three children and so does Edith," said Theodore, in a letter to Edith's mother. "Alice is worshiped by both of the boys. Kermit holds out his little arms to her whenever she comes near, and she really takes care of him like a little mother. Kermie is a darling little fellow, so soft and sweet. As for blessed Ted, he is just as much of a comfort as he ever was. When I come in to afternoon tea, he and Alice sidle hastily around to my chair, knowing that I will surreptitiously give them all the icing off the cake, if I can get Edith's attention attracted elsewhere. Every evening I have a wild romp with them."

The little house that Theodore had rented seemed cramped after Sagamore Hill, but, in addition to Rock Creek Park, there were a number of small parks and squares where the children could run and stretch their legs. "We used to be taken occasionally to play on the terrace of the Capitol," said Alice. "In those days the grounds of the White House were open to the public, and we played there, too."

Their father was also interested in the White House. Sometimes, walking along Pennsylvania Avenue on his way to work, he would glance toward the tall white pillars. Perhaps he was remembering what Bill Sewall had said. The idea that he might become President made his heart beat faster. Was it possible, just possible, that he would live in the White House some day?

He shook his head and walked on. He would do well, he thought, if he kept his present position as Civil Service Commissioner.

His duty in this office was to enforce the new Civil Service Act. For a long time, many government positions, such as clerks and letter carriers, had been given to members of the political party that had won the latest election. The Civil Service Act provided for a "merit system," and stated that such positions should be given to the men and women who did best on special examinations for each position that was open. Some of the political leaders, however, went right on recommending their own favorites for government jobs.

One day Theodore Roosevelt had a caller, a widow with two children. She told him that she had been employed for a number of years in a certain bureau in a department of the government, but was now out of work. She no longer had enough money even to buy food for her family. Years later Theodore Roosevelt told her story in his *Autobiography.*

The chief of the bureau had called her, he said, and told her he was very sorry that he had to dismiss her. She was much upset and asked why; she thought her work had been satisfactory. He said that she had indeed been doing well, and that he wished he could keep her, but that he could not because a certain Senator wanted her place for a friend. The Senator was an extremely influential man. His wants had to be attended to, and the woman had to go. And go she did.

Theodore found the woman another position, but he knew that there were many government workers who had not been treated fairly. One difficulty he faced was that most Americans did not know very much about Civil Service. So he wrote articles for magazines, and went about the country making speeches. Government positions were not "the property of politicians," he said. "They belonged to the people and should be filled only with regard to the needs of public service."

Sometimes he called in the newspaper reporters. As he strode up and down his office, he flung out his arms in wide gestures. He pounded one fist into his other hand. He nodded his head so vigorously that his glasses seemed about to fly off. Reporters who had once considered Civil Service a rather dull subject changed their minds. It was interesting, they decided, as they scribbled into their notebooks. That was because Theodore Roosevelt himself was so interesting.

But some of the politicians—the selfish ones—were furious. They wanted government jobs for friends who had helped them to get elected, and they demanded that Theodore Roosevelt be dismissed from his position. "I am perfectly willing to be turned out," he said, "but while in I mean business. When my duty is to enforce a law, that law is surely going to be enforced."

In the end he won out over his enemies. People throughout the United States, aroused by his speeches and magazine articles, wrote their Congressmen demanding further reforms. He had good reason to feel proud of his record, and the six years spent in Washington were happy ones for his family. Two new members were added. Ethel was not quite four and Archibald, or Archie, was a year old in the spring of 1895 when their father was offered another position in New York. The new mayor there wanted him to be a commissioner on the city Police Board.

"If I go," he wrote Bamie, who was then in Europe, "I must make up my mind to much criticism and disappointment. On the other hand, I am nearly through what I can do here. It was a rather close decision; but on the whole I felt I ought to go, though it is 'taking chances.'"

He did not mind taking chances. "It is impossible to win the great prizes of life," he once said, "without running risks."

11

There were four commissioners on the New York City Police Board at that time, and Theodore Roosevelt was elected president. As he sat at his desk at headquarters, he was busy with plans for reforming the Police Department. Certainly reforms were needed. He knew that many members of the police force were lazy or dishonest. They took bribes from thieves, gamblers, and other lawbreakers. These criminals, instead of being arrested, were protected by the police.

Even more to blame than the "crooked" policemen were the "crooked" politicians. They, too, received bribes—often very large sums of money—for protecting persons who broke the law. The political "bosses" had their own "system," and the police were told whom they could arrest and whom they couldn't. Honest men on the force who refused to take orders from the bosses were seldom promoted.

These conditions would have to be changed, thought the new commissioner grimly. He talked of his plans to Tom Byrnes, the Chief of Police.

The Chief looked at him with a thin smile. Byrnes had decided a long time before that the way to get ahead was to work under the "system." "It will break you, Mr. Roosevelt," he said. "You will yield. You are but human."

There were many people who agreed with the Chief. Even those who wanted an honest police force thought that nothing could be done about the crooked politicians. But not Jacob Riis. Riis was a reporter on a New York newspaper. Several years earlier he had written a book, *How the Other Half Lives,* that told about the poor people in the slums. Like many other well-to-do New Yorkers, Theodore was shocked by the book. He had assured Jacob Riis that he wanted to do whatever he could to help, and the two men became good friends.

The first night after Theodore became a police commissioner, he and Jacob took a long walk through the city streets. They came upon policemen who were asleep when they were supposed to be on duty. One policeman was sitting on the sidewalk reading a newspaper. He looked up in surprise to find a stranger with thick glasses and glistening white teeth glaring down at him.

"Why aren't you walking your beat?" the stranger barked.

"What's it to you?" the policeman replied. "Get on with you, or I'll run you in."

Then his jaw dropped open, as he recognized the commissioner.

Many nights after that Theodore Roosevelt walked the streets, sometimes with Jacob Riis, sometimes alone. He wanted to see for himself how the police were doing their duty.

The newspapers played up the story. "ALL POLICEMEN BEWARE!" read one headline. "HAROUN AL RASCHID IN NEW YORK" read another. Theodore chuckled. Perhaps he liked being compared with a character in the Arabian Nights story—the colorful ruler who had wandered through the city of Baghdad in disguise because he had wanted to talk with his people and find out about their problems. The newspaper writers called him Haroun Al Roosevelt.

They also called him "Teddy." Cartoonists drew funny pictures of him, showing his prominent white teeth and thick glasses. Peddlers walked up and down the streets selling "Teddy teeth." This toy could be placed between the lips, and there was a brown mustache attached. There were some men who thought it a good joke to walk up to a policeman and flash the teeth in his face, and the police were kept busy chasing the peddlers away. They also kept on the lookout for the owner of the real "Teddy teeth"—the new president of the Police Board.

"These midnight rambles are great fun," he wrote Bamie. "I make some rather startling discoveries at times. My work brings me in contact with every class of people in New York, and I get a real glimpse of the swarming millions. Finally, I do really feel that I am accomplishing a great deal. We are gradually having the laws better and better observed and getting more and more control over the force."

The honest policemen liked the new president. They could count on him to be fair. He praised the men who had done good work, and promoted them if they deserved to be promoted. The dishonest ones were afraid of him. If they neglected their duties, they knew that they might have to pay a fine or be suspended. It did not matter to him if they had friends among important politicians. Political "pull" meant nothing any more. Every policeman was expected to arrest criminals, no matter who they were. They were expected to help all law-abiding citizens who needed help.

The ones who needed the most help were the families in the slums. One of Theodore's duties was to serve as a member of the Health Board. With Jacob Riis he inspected many of the tenement houses in the poorer sections of the city. To his surprise he learned that some of the worst buildings were owned by wealthy men, who became even wealthier by charging high rents. Sometimes fourteen people had to live together in a single room. There was never enough light, or enough air, or enough water. The children had no place to play except in filthy streets and alleys.

"It is one thing to listen to tales of overcrowded tenements," said Theodore, "another to actually see what overcrowding means. There was a very hot spell one midsummer while I was Police Commissioner, and most of each night I spent walking through the tenement house districts to see what was being done. Every resource of the Health Department, of the Police Department, and even the Fire Department, which flooded the hot streets, was taxed in an effort to alleviate the suffering. Much of it was heartbreaking, especially the gasping misery of little children and worn-out mothers. It was a tragic week."

In his book Jacob Riis had told the people what was wrong in the slums. Theodore, working with the other members of the Health Board, tried to have the wrongs corrected. During the weeks and months that followed, city streets were cleaned. Doctors visited the schools and examined the pupils. Parks were laid out, and playgrounds opened. It was very important, thought Theodore, that boys and girls have a decent place to play.

They must also, as many of them as possible, have a decent place to live. He learned that there were certain laws about tenements that had never been enforced. Jacob Riis made a list of the six worst buildings, and the Health Board ordered them to be torn down.

Theodore knew that many other reforms were needed. New laws should be passed. But a start had been made. "I tried faithfully to do what Father would have done," he once told Jacob Riis.

The kind, bearded gentleman, the hero of his childhood, was often in his thoughts. What would Father have advised? was a question he asked himself again and again. Meanwhile he was trying to be as wise a parent as the first Theodore had been. One "melancholy feature" of his work, as he wrote Bamie, was that he did not see as much of his children as he wished.

"In the morning I get little more than a glimpse of them," he said.

"In the evening I always take a romp with Archie, who loves me with all his small silly heart; the two little boys (Ted and Kermit) usually look over what they call my 'jewel box' while I am dressing; I then play with cunning Ethel in her crib; and Alice takes dinner with us."

Often he was too busy to get home for dinner. He stayed in town overnight or caught the last train for Oyster Bay. Then he would ride his bicycle the three miles between the station and the house. As he pedaled through the darkness or under a sky studded with stars, his heart lifted. At Sagamore Hill Edith, "sweetest and best of wives and mothers," was waiting. Ethel, "a little scamp," but "too attractive for anything" and Archie, the baby, would be asleep. Alice, Ted, and Kermit might still be lying awake, listening for his step on the veranda. Or perhaps they were making plans for next Saturday, hoping he would be home in time to take them on a picnic.

Like the children, Theodore always looked forward to the days he could spend with his family.

12

Even his free days at Sagamore Hill were busy. Theodore was working hard to finish the fourth volume of *The Winning of the West*, but he still found time for the children. Three other families of Roosevelts lived close by, and there were sixteen young cousins who played together. The morning after his return home usually found him wearing knickerbockers and tramping through the woods, followed by a long line of youngsters of various ages and sizes.

"To be with him was to have fun," one cousin, Nicholas Roosevelt, remembered, "because of the humor, cheerfulness, and warm affection. We loved nothing more than the games of hide-and-seek in the old barn at Sagamore Hill, the overnight camping trips, and the family picnics. No matter how much sand was in the clams or how lukewarm the ginger ale or how burned the steaks, he enjoyed each picnic, more even than the youngsters."

The mothers did not always share his enthusiasm. They preferred their food properly cooked. Sometimes they were downright angry. One very cold day "Cousin Theodore" allowed the children to wade through a pond, and they came back shivering. At Sagamore Hill, Edith marched Alice, Ted, and Kermit upstairs, to be given big doses of quinine. Kermit slipped away for a word with his father.

"Please don't let Mother give me that awful medicine," he begged.

"Kermit," Theodore replied, "I'll be lucky if she doesn't make me take some of the stuff, too."

And later he admitted to one of the young relatives, "Your Cousin Edith sometimes treats me as her oldest and rather worst child."

He was joking, of course, but perhaps it was because he *did* act like a child sometimes that he was so much fun. One day he and some of the youngsters climbed a tall tree. It was hollow, with an opening some twenty feet from the ground. Theodore had brought a rope, which he tied around the waist of each child in turn. Then down, down, the child felt himself being lowered into a deep dark hole. It was both scary and thrilling to be down there all alone.

Cousin Theodore was always thinking of something interesting to do—something different. One of his games was called "Point-to-Point" or "Obstacle Race." The players agreed on some landmark—a certain tree, perhaps—and started toward it, walking in a straight line. No matter what obstacle lay in their path, they were not supposed to turn aside. If they came to a pond, they waded or swam across. If a haystack was in the way, they burrowed through it or climbed over it.

"Over and above, never around," Theodore would shout, and no excuses were permitted.

"His teachings were simple," said Nicholas, "to overcome fear, to finish what we set out to do, to play the game well and hard, to shun excuses, to be loyal and to be truthful."

Another delightfully scary experience was the race down Cooper's Bluff, a high sand bank rising from the edge of the bay. The children clasped hands and, with Theodore in the lead, ran down the steep slope, rolling, tumbling, to the bottom. When the tide was in, they often found themselves up to their waists in water.

The Roosevelts liked to swim. Theodore taught the children simply by dumping them overboard from the float a short distance from the shore. Bathing suits looked very different in those days. The boys wore tights. Edith's outfit had a full skirt, worn over long pantalettes. Theodore's suit was a one-piece red garment buttoned down the front. One afternoon he hung it on the side of the bathhouse to dry. The bright splotch of color made an excellent target, when Ted and some of his cousins decided to practice with his new rifle.

"Next day," said Ted, "Father went in bathing with Mother and some of her friends. The bathing suit was new and Father was proud of it. While standing on the float he called on the company to admire it. They looked at it, and found that the seat of the trousers was punctured with a series of holes like the bottom of a sieve."

Sometimes Teddy, Monroe, and Corinne Robinson came out from New York for a visit. They were the children of the first Corinne, Theodore's younger sister. Elliott's daughter, Eleanor, came the summer she was eleven. Her father had died, and she was very sad. She also felt awkward and shy with her lively relatives. No one would have guessed then that some day she was going to be one of the world's most famous women.

"Poor little soul, she is very plain," said her Aunt Edith, "but the ugly duckling may turn out to be a swan."

She was thinking of the fairy tale by Hans Christian Andersen. But Eleanor, unlike the ugly duckling in the story, could not swim. When her Uncle Ted ducked her, she was frightened. She was terrified the first time she joined in a race down Cooper's Bluff. When she tried it again, she found it rather thrilling. The picnics and camping trips reminded her of the stories that Elliott, her father, had liked to tell.

He had often talked about the first Theodore Roosevelt. One Thanksgiving he had taken her to visit the Newsboys' Lodging House, the clubhouse that her grandfather had started. He was a joyful man who had brought much joy to others. Perhaps it was the same keen enjoyment of living in her Uncle Ted that drew Eleanor to him. She never forgot the bright summer days at Sagamore Hill.

"I remember these visits as a great joy in some ways," she said later. "I loved chasing through the haystacks in the barn with Uncle Ted after us. And going up to the gun room on the top floor where Uncle Ted would read aloud, chiefly poetry."

Theodore Roosevelt read poetry with the same enthusiasm that he did everything else. And when he talked about some incident in American history, he made it seem so real it was hard to realize that he had not been there himself.

Some of the adventures he described were his own.

"Father often told us tales of his ranch and the West," said Ted. "Shuddering with delicious excitement, we heard of thieves and grizzly bears."

Both parents liked to read aloud, often from the same books they had read when they were young.

The young Roosevelts liked pets as much as their father had. Guinea pigs, flying squirrels, a badger, and a bear shared the spacious grounds with dogs and horses and a number of farm animals. The cows and pigs and chickens each had its own name, and the children made friends of them all. Their favorite pet was another Pony Grant, named after the pony their father had ridden as a boy.

One day Ted was hugging his forelegs, when the gentle little beast decided that Ted's straw hat looked good enough to eat. He began munching on the brim. At this Ted let out "a wail of anguish," said Theodore, "evidently thinking the pony had decided to treat him like a radish."

Perhaps no father ever had a better time with his children than did Theodore Roosevelt. They helped him to forget his worries; and he had many worries during the two years that he served as president of the New York Police Board.

Many people thought him too strict because he insisted that the so-called "Sunday law" should be enforced. This law stated that saloons must be closed on Sundays, and the police had seen to it that some of the saloons *were* kept closed. Other saloonkeepers who bribed the dishonest politicians and policemen had been allowed to stay open.

"I am enforcing honestly," said Theodore, "a law that hitherto had been enforced dishonestly."

If the people did not approve of the law, he declared, they could ask the State Legislature in Albany to change it. Unless it was changed, it must be obeyed—not just by some of the saloonkeepers, but by all of them. That was only fair; bribery must be stopped.

Finally his enemies decided to have a mammoth parade to show how much they disliked his policy. Thousands of people marched down Lexington Avenue. Others rode on bicycles, on horseback, and on gaily decorated floats. As a joke the president of the Police Board had been invited to attend. No one thought that he would come.

But he did come. As the paraders passed the reviewing stand, some of them glanced up in surprise. A man with large white teeth and eye-glasses was grinning down at them.

"Why, it's Teddy—Teddy Roosevelt," someone shouted.

"Where's Teddy? I want to see Teddy," said someone else.

Theodore smiled good-naturedly. He kept on smiling, even when someone hissed. He was being such a good sport that most of the paraders could not help but admire him.

"What's the matter with Roosevelt?" someone cried.

Hundreds of voices replied, "He's—all—right."

It took two hours for the parade to pass the reviewing stand, and Theodore was cheered again and again. "I enjoyed it greatly," he told reporters, "but one hundred parades will not cause me to move one inch in doing my duty. The law is on the books, and it will be enforced as rigidly as it ever was."

The crooked politicians and dishonest policemen were in despair. No longer could they collect large sums of money from wealthy saloon-keepers by permitting them to break the law. Senator Thomas Platt, the boss of the Republican Party in New York State, and his friends, decided that Theodore Roosevelt had to go. The State Legislature was asked to pass a law abolishing, or doing away with, the position that he held.

"They will make a resolute effort to legislate me out of office," he wrote Bamie. "I rather doubt if they will succeed. Under the old system, classes of criminals were protected. Now we protect no criminal, and in consequence the war we wage is very hard. I work and fight from dawn until dark, but at bottom I know that the work has been well worth doing. On the whole I am prouder of it than of any work I ever did."

He was proud but also rather sad. An ambitious young man, he knew that he might never have a chance to hold another political office. "All the party bosses will oppose me," he told a friend. "I realized this when I began to fight for the enforcement of the Sunday law and against police bribery. But it was the only course I could honestly pursue, and I am willing to abide by the consequences."

He was wrong about one thing. His political career was not over. In the spring of 1897, the new President, William McKinley, asked him to be Assistant Secretary of the Navy, and he returned to Washington.

Theodore was happy in his new position. He was happier still that November, when another son, Quentin, was born.

"The merriest, jolliest baby imaginable," Edith described him.

"Nothing else takes the place, or can take the place of family life," said Theodore.

13

I**N HIS** new position, Theodore Roosevelt was determined to build up a stronger Navy. It worried him that the nation was not better prepared, if war should come. And he was convinced that it *was* coming— war with Spain.

For many years the island of Cuba had been a Spanish colony. When the Cubans revolted, Spanish soldiers had arrived to put down the rebellion. Stories of their cruelty were printed in many American newspapers, and the American people felt very sorry for the Cubans.

President McKinley and the Secretary of the Navy hoped to avoid war. The Secretary's new assistant had no use for this point of view. He believed that the government should send armed forces into Cuba to drive the Spaniards out.

"I very deeply felt that it was our duty to free Cuba," he said.

The majority of Americans agreed. Then in February 1898, newspapers from coast to coast printed a piece of news that seemed to set their hearts on fire. A United States battleship, the *Maine*, while on a visit to Cuba, had been blown up and sunk. Two hundred and sixty sailors on the ship were killed. What really caused the explosion is still a mystery, but at that time most Americans blamed the Spaniards.

"Remember the *Maine!*" read the headlines in the newspapers.

"Remember the *Maine!*" shouted the people. The President finally gave in to their demands and asked Congress to declare war against Spain. Cuba was declared to be free and independent.

Theodore's decision had been made weeks before. If war came he wanted to have a part in the fighting. The President and the Secretary of the Navy reminded him that he was doing good work where he was, but Theodore believed people should practice what they preached.

"I have done all I could to bring on this war," he told Jacob Riis. "Now that it has come, I have no business to ask others to do the fighting and stay at home myself."

The Secretary of War offered to make Theodore the colonel of the First United States Volunteer Cavalry, but he realized that he had not had enough military experience. He asked to be made lieutenant-colonel instead, and his friend Leonard Wood became the colonel.

Old Harvard friends, Eastern college boys and athletes, policemen who had served under him in New York, ranchmen and cowboys, and even a few Indians, all of whom wanted to serve in his regiment, gathered in San Antonio, Texas, for a month of training. Here high-spirited Westerners, although they had prided themselves on never taking orders, marched and drilled. The "swells," as the Westerners called the Eastern college boys, peeled mountains of potatoes while on kitchen duty. Because most of the men were skilled horseback riders from the West, the regiment was nicknamed "the Rough Riders."

"You've got to perform without flinching whatever duty is assigned you," Theodore told them. "Regardless of the danger and no matter what comes, you must not squeal."

The men drew a deep breath. They knew that their lieutenant-colonel would never ask anything of them that he would not ask of himself. He was proving to be a good leader, and they were devoted to him.

In his tent at night, perhaps Theodore's thoughts went back to the books he had read as a boy. His favorite people in history had always been leaders. They had always been brave. Like them, he and his Rough Riders must be brave when he led them into battle.

The chance to test their bravery soon came. The Rough Riders were among several thousand American troops that landed on the Cuban coast toward the end of June. That night they camped a quarter of a mile from shore. The next morning came an order from the general in command that they were to join other American forces and advance on the enemy.

The hot sun beat down. Not a breath of air stirred, and the men were sweating as they made their way along the jungle paths. Sometimes the Americans came out into a clearing and passed deserted plantations. All Cuba seemed to be deserted, except for the birds that sang in the treetops, exactly as if there were no war.

"Where are them Spaniards?" asked one Rough Rider plaintively.

At that moment a shot rang out—then another and another. There was the sound of firing all around them.

Theodore, although very excited at first, grew calmer as the danger increased. His men were creeping through a thicket, rising now and then to rush forward a few feet. When more shots rang out, they fell to the ground again. Slowly, inch by inch, they advanced a mile and a half. To their left, members of another battalion were crawling through the tall grass. When their commander was wounded, Colonel Wood ordered Theodore to take command. He now had a much larger number of soldiers in his charge.

He rose cautiously and looked around. A bullet pierced the trunk of the tree by which he was standing. His eyes and one ear were filled with splinters, but he was not really hurt. From his new position he

could see a hill in the distance. On the hill were a group of ranch houses with red-tiled roofs. At last he knew where the Spaniards were.

He gave an order to advance. As the Americans rushed forward, the enemy was taken by surprise and, after a short fight, beat a hasty retreat. Theodore was very sad about the loss of sixteen of his men but proud of their bravery.

"Every man behaved well," he wrote Corinne afterwards. "There was no flinching."

After that battle Colonel Wood was promoted and became a general. Theodore, who had proved his ability to command, was made a full colonel. A week later, mounted on a horse named Texas, he led the Rough Riders into the fight that was to make them famous. Side by side with the Tenth Regiment of Regulars, a Negro regiment, they stormed up a steep hill where the Spaniards were entrenched at the top. "The Battle of San Juan Hill" the reporters called it when they sent the story to their newspapers back home. Like thousands of other

Americans, the family at Sagamore Hill read about the gallant charge.

"When they came to the open smooth hillside," one newspaper said, "there was no protection. Bullets were raining down at them. There was a moment's hesitation. Then came the order from Colonel Roosevelt: 'Forward! Forward!' Out into the open the men went, and up the hill. Up they went with the colored troops alongside them, not a man flinching. Roosevelt was a hundred feet in the lead. He sat erect on his horse, holding his sword and shouting for his men to follow him. Finally his horse was shot from under him, but he landed on his feet and continued calling for his men to advance. He charged up the hill afoot. . . . At last the position was won. The Spaniards still could have annihilated the Americans, but the Yankees' daring dazed them. They turned and ran."

The Rough Riders were thrilled by their part in the victory. There was a song they liked to sing:

"Rough, rough, we're the stuff,
We want to fight, and we can't get enough,
Whoo-pee!"

Fortunately the war was soon over. By the middle of July the Spaniards were ready to surrender. But hard days lay ahead for the Americans. Four thousand soldiers were sick with malaria or yellow fever, and more of them died from disease than had been killed in battle. Although Colonel Roosevelt kept well, he felt heartsick for his men. He grew more and more impatient as the days passed and no ships arrived to take them home. Army doctors said that more than half of the soldiers might die unless they could be moved to a cooler, more healthful climate.

Something had to be done. The leaders in the War Department back in Washington did not seem to understand how bad conditions were. A soldier is not supposed to criticize his superiors, but Colonel Roosevelt decided that saving the lives of his men was more important than obeying a rule of military etiquette. Several other officers backed him up, and they wrote a letter to their commander in Cuba.

"This army must be moved at once, or perish," the letter warned. "The persons responsible for preventing such a move will be responsible for the unnecessary loss of many thousands of lives."

The commander showed the letter to an American reporter, who promptly sent a cable about it to his newspaper. Within a few days, the story was being printed throughout the United States. Although the War Department had already sent an order to Cuba that the troops were to return home, the newspapers gave Colonel Roosevelt most of the credit. It had been a brave thing, people said, for him to lead the charge up San Juan Hill. It had been an even finer thing to stand up for his men.

The suggestion had been made in a number of newspaper editorials that Colonel Roosevelt would make an excellent governor for New York State. Senator Platt, the Republican boss, and his friends, did not care for the idea, but many voters were tired of the way their state government was being managed. During the past few years the taxpayers' money had been shamefully wasted. They knew that Theodore Roosevelt was honest. He had courage. Nearly every day since the battle of San Juan Hill, there had been a new story about him on the front page. He was probably the most popular man in America that hot August afternoon when his ship docked at Montauk Point on the eastern tip of Long Island.

The colonel, standing on the bridge, lifted his field glasses to his eyes. A shout went up from the shore, where a crowd had gathered to welcome the soldiers. On shipboard the band was playing as the brown-jeaned men crowded to the rail. When the gangplank was lowered, the colonel was the first man ashore. Immediately he was surrounded by reporters.

They wanted to know if he was going to run for governor, but that was a question he was not yet ready to answer. He grinned and turned away to greet his old friend Jacob Riis. Other friends and army officers pressed close to shake his hand.

"Colonel Roosevelt was the happiest man on the dock," wrote one reporter. "He was like a boy home from school for a long vacation—just like a boy who had thrown his lessons to the winds. He gossiped and laughed in great glee. He good-naturedly refused to talk politics."

Meanwhile the Rough Riders, who were to stay here with thousands of other soldiers, until they could be mustered out, were forming in a double file on the beach for the march to their quarters. Those too ill to walk rode in ambulances drawn by army mules. That night every man slept on a comfortable cot, and had a canvas roof over his head. He had fresh water to drink. He had good food and plenty of it. And in a few weeks he would be going home!

For Colonel Roosevelt there was time for a brief visit to Sagamore Hill and a happy reunion with his family. Then on learning that some more of his men had been taken ill, he cut short his leave and hurried back to camp. "My place is with the boys," he said.

14

Soon after Colonel Roosevelt arrived at Montauk Point, a man named Lemuel Quigg appeared at the door of his tent. He had come at the request of Thomas Platt.

"There is a good deal of talk about your being our next governor," Mr. Quigg explained. "Senator Platt has asked me to find out, if the Republicans should nominate you, would you accept?"

This time Theodore did not hesitate. "I'd be delighted," he said.

Lemuel Quigg pursed his lips. Both men realized that Senator Platt did not like the independent young colonel. They also knew that the coming election was going to be a close one, and the Republicans could not hope to win without a popular candidate. They needed Colonel Roosevelt.

"I hope you get the nomination," said Mr. Quigg. "I believe the nominating convention will want you, but I don't need to tell you that Thomas Platt is boss. He wishes to know, if you are elected, would you ask his advice? Or would you—well, would you make war on him and his friends?"

Theodore looked startled. "I would not want to make war on Mr. Platt or anybody else," he said. "Certainly I would ask his advice, just as I would ask advice of others who might be able to help me. However, after considering the advice carefully—" he paused between each word—"I would have to let my own conscience guide me. I would have to do what I myself thought was best for the public good."

Mr. Quigg rose to leave. "I think that is all anybody could expect," he replied. "I shall tell Senator Platt what you have said."

What wonderful good fortune he had had, thought Theodore. Both as Civil Service Commissioner and as president of the New York Police Board he had done a hard job and done it well. He had come through a war unhurt, and now he was a popular hero. But could his good fortune last? The election for governor was going to be a close one.

"Do you think I should try?" he asked a friend. "Up to now I have had a wonderful time, but I may have reached the crest of the wave. What if I begin to go down? I may fail, you know."

"Pshaw!" the friend replied. "My political opinion isn't worth much, but I know you're headed for big things."

The Rough Riders agreed. Several of the men who had been lawyers and politicians in their Western states offered to stay on in New York to help in Theodore Roosevelt's election campaign. On the morning that the regiment was to be mustered out of service, there was a feeling of gaiety in camp, but it was gaiety tinged with sadness. Wonderful friendships had been formed in the hot Cuban jungles. It was going to be hard to say good-by, especially to the colonel.

The men gathered on the plain, just out of sight of his tent, where they were joined by about two hundred Negro soldiers who had fought beside them at San Juan Hill. Together with other spectators—doctors, nurses, and officers from other regiments—they formed a hollow square. In the center of this square stood a table, on which there was a bulky object covered with a blanket. An officer went to the colonel's tent and asked him to come out.

Theodore was surprised to see such a large crowd. The bulky object, when it was uncovered, proved to be a bronze statue, "The Bronco Buster," and reminded him of his Western days. He was deeply moved when it was presented to him as a gift from his Rough Riders.

"I would rather have my position as your colonel than any other position on earth," he told them.

As, one by one, the men filed past to say good-by, he recalled some adventure they had shared or some amusing incident. Many of them were laughing as they shook hands. Colonel Roosevelt was as eager as any of his men to return home. When he arrived at Sagamore Hill one golden September afternoon, the children had made a sign that announced in big, bold letters: IN HONOR OF COLONEL ROOSEVELT'S RETURN. They rushed to meet him. Ted, now eleven years old, and looking like a smaller copy of his father, gazed up adoringly through thick-lensed spectacles. Kermit and Ethel threw their arms around him. Edith was holding Quentin, the ten-month-old baby. Archie, aged four, and too young to know what war meant, seemed to think that his father had been on a hunting trip.

"Did you bring me a bear?" he asked.

"No, but I have an eagle for you," Theodore replied. "It was the mascot of our regiment, and one of my men is bringing it from camp. Yes, and he's bringing Texas, too."

"Texas? The horse you rode at San Juan Hill?" asked Ted, his voice squeaking in excitement. "May I ride him, Father?"

"Certainly—if you can. He's a rather cross old bronco."

That night Theodore Roosevelt put his uniform away. The next morning he was wearing his old gray woolen knickerbockers and a comfortable shirt as he started through the woods for a long hike. The children would hardly let him out of their sight. When the bald-headed eagle arrived, it was added to their menagerie of pets. Texas was a hero in their eyes, but when Ted tried to ride him he found that his father was right. The horse *was* cross. Sometimes it would rear and go over backwards, and Ted would find himself sprawled on the ground. Or it would dash off into the underbrush, and he would be scraped off its back by overhanging branches.

Even better than having the two new pets was being able to meet some of the Rough Riders who came to visit. Nor were they the only ones who wanted to see their old commander. A constant stream of callers—friends, politicians, and reporters—made their way up the winding road that led to Sagamore Hill. Hundreds of letters arrived from admirers and had to be answered.

He was even busier after the state Republican convention met in late September and nominated him for governor. The night that Theodore Roosevelt made his first campaign speech, at Carnegie Hall in New York City, there was such a large crowd outside the building that it took him ten minutes to fight his way through.

"This is nearly as bad as the charge up San Juan Hill," he said good-naturedly.

"Hurrah for Teddy!" the crowd shouted.

A few days later he and seven of his Rough Riders boarded a special train to begin a tour of the state. In every town where he spoke during the next three weeks hundreds of people came to hear him. They wanted to see the hero they had read about in their newspapers. They cheered the Rough Riders who sat behind him on the platform.

In spite of this enthusiasm, Theodore felt discouraged when he returned to Oyster Bay early in November. The majority of voters might like him, but they decidedly did not like the way his party had been managing their state government during the past few years. When he went to bed on election night, he thought that he had lost.

A loud ringing of the doorbell aroused him from sleep. It rang again, echoing through the silent house. The older children heard it and sat up in bed. Their father heard it, got up, and put on a red dressing gown. He lighted a kerosene lamp and trudged sleepily downstairs. He opened the door to find a reporter standing on the porch.

"Congratulations, Governor."

"Governor?" asked Theodore.

"Yes, you have been elected," the reporter informed him. "Elected by nearly 18,000 majority."

"Why, that's bully!" Theodore replied.

The children were thrilled. They would be moving to Albany, the state capital, at the end of the year, and during the next few weeks they saw more of their father than they had for a long time. He played bear with Archie and baby Quentin. He took Ethel and the older boys on long hikes. With the first snow he brought out their toboggan, and they skimmed down the slick, white slopes. As usual, they were looking forward to Christmas, but Theodore Roosevelt, the governor-elect, had other children to think about besides his own.

One day he received a letter from a boy in Miss Satterie's school for Italian children. This was the same school, managed by the Children's Aid Society, in which his father had been so interested.

"Dear Colonel Roosevelt," the letter read, "will you come to see us children before you go to Albany? We want to see you very much. Please, please do come. Our teacher is Miss Satterie. Please do not tell her that I write you, for she told us not to worry you. Us boys are glad you are going to be Governor."

Theodore Roosevelt did not mind the mistakes in the letter. A few days later he was knocking on a classroom door. When it was opened he saw the same Miss Satterie who had been teaching there for more than thirty years.

There was a shout from her pupils: "Teddy! Teddy! Teddy's here."

The teacher started to apologize, but her famous visitor stopped her. "It's all right; Teddy's my name," he said. Then he turned to the class. "What would you like me to talk about?" he asked.

"About the Rough Riders," said one boy.

95

"About your horse Texas," said another.

The colonel flashed them a smile. "Oh, yes, my horse Texas. The papers said that he was shot from under me at San Juan Hill, but he wasn't really shot, you know. He was grazed by bullets, and when we came to the first wire fence I had to jump off and let Texas go. I never expected to see him again, but when the fight was over Texas was found. He was not hurt to speak of, and was really as good as ever."

He went on to tell the class what "a corking good regiment" the Rough Riders were. One of his bravest soldiers was the bugler. During their first battle, his hand was wounded and he could no longer hold the bugle. But after his hand was bandaged he went back and helped to take care of other wounded soldiers. This young man—like most of the children in the school—had been born in Italy.

A sigh ran through the room. The pupils, their soft dark eyes on the speaker, were so interested that they forgot to applaud. They were feeling very proud.

Theodore Roosevelt also felt proud. As he turned to leave, he noticed a photograph on Miss Satterie's desk. It was a picture of his father, who was still honored in this school. "He was the finest man I ever knew," said Theodore softly.

A few days later the governor-elect took part in a Christmas party at another school. Ever since he and Edith had moved to Oyster Bay, it had been their custom to give a Christmas tree to the Cove School and to provide presents for everyone. This year Ted and Kermit were among the pupils. When they filed into the room with the others, they saw their parents sitting on the platform behind the teacher.

During the program the children kept glancing toward the two Christmas trees sparkling with tinsel. The branches were loaded with candy and small packages, and larger gifts had been placed underneath on the floor. Nearly every boy and girl had either memorized a "piece" to recite or had a song to sing.

Finally a boy named James Gallagher walked to the front of the room. Jimmy's poem told of the brave deeds of a hero, a Rough Rider, named Theodore Roosevelt. It ended with the words:

"We'll send you to the White House
For the gallant deeds you've done."

There was loud applause, and Theodore's cheeks were still flushed when he gave out the presents. He would glance at a card, and call a name. Jimmy Gallagher received a shiny pair of skates.

Late that afternoon the Roosevelt family rode home in the sleigh. This was really their farm wagon. The wheels had been taken off and the body of the wagon placed on runners. It was cozy all snuggled down together in the straw, as the horses dashed up the winding road. Sleigh bells tinkled in the frosty air. The branches of trees, heavy with snow, were white against a darkening sky, and the lights of Sagamore gleamed faintly in the distance. In another week they would be leaving it. At that moment parents and childı ı alike may have felt a little homesick.

And yet they looked forward to living in Albany. And after Albany? Perhaps they were remembering the last two lines of Jimmy's poem.

15

THE FLAG-DRAPED Executive Chamber in Albany was filled with people when the new governor took his place on the platform. Behind him sat Edith and Alice. Ted and the younger children were in the gallery, and to their delight their father waved to them. They waved back, then leaned forward in their seats to listen when he began his speech.

"It is not given to any man," he said, "to see with absolutely clear vision into the future. All that can be done is to face the facts as we find them, to meet each difficulty in practical fashion." He promised that he would "strive steadily" to make conditions better for the people.

It was such a solemn moment that Edith felt close to tears. Alice, who was almost as tall as her father, looked very dignified. Ethel and her brothers applauded as loudly as anybody in the audience.

When they returned to the Executive Mansion they explored it from the cellar to the billiard room on the top floor. It was the biggest house they had ever lived in. Soon they felt as much at home there as they had at Sagamore Hill. They played many of the same games, and they still kept pets. When people in Albany learned that they liked animals, new ones kept arriving. They were kept in the cellar, where the children fed and tended them. This cellar was under the parlor, and during the cold weather all went well.

Then came the first warm day of spring, and the windows had to be opened to give the animals air. That afternoon while Mrs. Roosevelt was entertaining callers, she noticed a strange odor. She sniffed suspiciously; the parlor smelled exactly like a zoo. The young Roosevelts were told that they would have to give away some of their pets. This was a disappointment, but the fact that now they could see their father nearly every day made up for it.

Busy though he was, he found time to play with them. He liked his new home as much as the children did. He liked being governor. "There is a great deal of difficulty and of worry," he said, "but there is a chance to do good work and after all that is the main thing."

He had known from the beginning how hard the work would be. Some rich business men were in the habit of giving large sums of money to both Democrats and Republicans before election time. Then whichever party was elected, the business men felt safe. They felt sure that only the laws they wanted would be passed. Senator Platt, the Republican boss, told the Republican members of the legislature how they should vote. He also expected to tell the Republican governor what to do.

Much as Theodore Roosevelt disliked this way of managing a government, he saw the need to be a practical politician. He knew that he could accomplish more if Senator Platt felt friendly toward him. Besides he had agreed, before he was nominated, to ask advice.

"He kept his promise," the Senator admitted ruefully. "He *did* ask my advice. Then he did just what he pleased."

That was not exactly true. Theodore often took Thomas Platt's advice—if he thought the advice was good. Even when he refused, he tried to be polite. Senator Platt was also polite, at least for a while.

The new governor was especially interested in conservation. He had loved the outdoors ever since he was a boy, and he did not think that forests existed just to be cut down. Too often in the past, trees had been wasted when cut into logs by men who only wanted to make money. No new seeds had been planted. This meant that unless something was done there would be no trees for future generations. Not only in New York but throughout the nation, government officials had given away millions of acres of public land—and all because a few greedy rich men wanted to be even richer.

Governor Roosevelt was indignant. He felt that the forests and minerals and other natural resources in New York should be preserved for the people of the state. He wanted laws passed for the sensible protection of all harmless wild things, especially song birds.

"I was able to do a good deal for forest preservation and protection of our wild life," he was to write in his *Autobiography*. "All that later I strove for in the nation in connection with conservation was foreshadowed by what I strove to obtain for New York State while governor."

A number of other reforms were made. Among the laws he suggested was one limiting the number of hours that certain kinds of laborers could work in any one day. Another law provided that factories must protect their workers from dangerous machinery. Before Theodore Roosevelt became governor, many people in the state had not known how bad conditions were, but he called in the reporters and told them what he hoped to accomplish. Perhaps what he *said* was more important than what he *did*. He had a way of talking that made people sit up and take notice.

He talked entirely too much to please Senator Platt. Both of them soon realized that on more important matters they could never agree. The Senator's chief interest was in helping the wealthy men who managed the big corporations. The new governor was interested in *all* of the people.

On one occasion Senator Platt insisted that a certain man, who had been holding a position in the state government, be appointed again. Theodore was convinced that the man was not honest, and refused. A friend of Mr. Platt's asked the governor to meet him downtown.

"Governor," the man warned, "the Senator is going to win this fight. If you do what he wants, everything will be made easy for you. If you refuse, you will never hold another political office."

There was a long pause. Theodore hoped, when his term as governor was over, to be elected again. He realized that Senator Platt might be able to ruin his chances, but he shook his head.

"You have made up your mind?" the friend asked. "You know it means your ruin."

"Well, we will see about that. Good night."

The governor rose to leave. "Hold on," said Senator Platt's friend. "Appoint the man you want. The Senator will not oppose you."

Theodore breathed a sigh of relief. He remembered an old West African proverb that he liked: "Speak softly and carry a big stick." That was what he had tried to do. He would continue to treat Senator Platt with courtesy, but he would also hold his own. He was discovering that it took as much courage to be governor (as he later wrote his old friend, Bill Sewall) as to lead a charge up San Juan Hill.

As the end of his term approached, he realized how much his courage might cost him. The political bosses considered him a "dangerous" man—dangerous because he refused to do what they wanted. They were determined that he should not be nominated for governor a second time, but he was so popular that they did not dare come out against him openly.

"Why not kick him upstairs?" suggested Senator Platt.

What he meant was, "Why not find our troublesome governor a better position *outside* of the state?" The Republicans would be holding their national convention in June 1900, to nominate a President and Vice President for the next four years. William McKinley was almost certain to be nominated again for President. Why not, Platt argued, try to nominate Roosevelt for Vice President? If elected, he would have a dignified position but one with very little power. The Republican boss and his friends in New York State would then have a better chance to elect a governor who would do as he was told.

At that time the Vice President's principal duty was to preside over the Senate in the nation's capital, and Theodore was not interested in a position that would give him so little to do.

Then to his dismay many people in the Western states began to work for his nomination. Thousands had read about his bravery as colonel of the Rough Riders. They knew what he had done as governor, and they looked up to him as a new leader in the new century that was just beginning. By June, when the Republican convention opened in Philadelphia, he knew that he could have the nomination if he wanted it.

But did he want it? Some of his friends were convinced that he might be nominated for the Presidency in 1904. If he became Vice President in the meantime, would the voters of the country stop thinking of him for the higher office?

One day, sitting in a hotel room with his sister Corinne, Theodore talked about his problem.

He realized why Platt and his friends were urging his nomination. But he also had to consider the people who wanted him because they liked him. There was real enthusiasm for him in the West and in the Middle West. What was he to do? he asked his sister.

Before she could answer, the door opened. Three men carrying fife and drum and bugle marched in at the head of a line of delegates from Kansas. "We want Teddy; we want Teddy," they chanted, as they marched around and around the room. Theodore held up his hand for silence.

"Gentlemen," he said, "I know that you want what is best for the country and what you think is best for me. But, my friends, I *want* another term as governor. I am sure I could be of more use to my country as governor of New York State than as Vice President. I wish you would help me to do the thing which I think is best to do."

The only answer the delegates made was to repeat the singsong chant: "We want Teddy; we want Teddy." The same words could be heard again and again as they marched down the corridor. Theodore looked at his sister in despair, but had to laugh.

"What can I do with such people, Conie?" he asked. "What can I do?"

What he finally did was to let the Kansas delegation and others like them have their own way. When William McKinley was nominated again for President, Theodore seconded the nomination. Edith, sitting in the gallery, was thrilled by the burst of applause that followed his speech. The bands played, and delegates from different states marched up and down the aisles. There was laughter as a stuffed elephant was carried to the platform. Finally the chairman rose and raised his hand for silence. He asked for nominations for Vice President, and Theodore Roosevelt's name was presented.

"Yip-yip-hooray!" The shouts were so loud they seemed to shake the rafters of the building. Bands played and delegates tossed their hats into the air. They sang and marched up and down the aisles again. Soon it was all over. Edith, pale but smiling, heard her husband proclaimed the candidate for Vice President of the United States. It was not what she had wanted for him; not what he had wanted for himself. But perhaps it was for the best, and he had been paid a great compliment.

"Nothing can keep you from doing good work wherever you are," one of his friends wrote him, "nor from getting lots of fun out of it."

AFTER HIS nomination, Theodore Roosevelt traveled from coast to coast and made several hundred speeches. In July he spoke in Oklahoma at a reunion of the Rough Riders, where the men who had served under him in Cuba cheered lustily for their colonel. Later, in Dakota, he met some of the old friends he had known during his ranching days, and they felt a special pride in his accomplishments.

Theodore returned their affection. In the town of Bismarck, from the rear platform of his train, he talked to a large audience. "I had studied a lot about men and things before I saw you fellows," he told them, "but it was only when I came here that I began to know anything or measure men rightly."

When the train moved on to Medora, he found a crowd of forty or fifty people waiting to welcome him. Some of them hung back shyly, but in an instant the candidate for Vice President was among them shaking hands. One man who pushed through the crowd was grinning. It was George Myer, who had once done the cooking at Chimney Butte.

"Do you remember the time I made green biscuits for you?" he asked.

Theodore chuckled. "I do, I do," he said. "The best proof in the world that I have good health is that I ate your cooking and survived."

With nearly everyone he met, he had some memory to share. He and Joe Ferris talked about their first buffalo hunt. Another man approached leading a horse. Would Mr. Roosevelt like to take a ride?

Mr. Roosevelt certainly would. He jumped on the bronco's back and galloped along one of the trails that he remembered so well. It felt good to see those jagged buttes, gray and strangely beautiful, rising against a cloudless sky. It was good to be among his old friends, and to know that they wished him well in the coming election.

"It does not seem right," he told them just before his train pulled out, "that I should come here and not stay."

As he traveled westward, he was gaining new friends as well, thousands of them. Crowds gathered at every railroad station where his train stopped. In Portland, Oregon, a number of Western governors gave a dinner in his honor. Governor John Brady of Alaska came up to shake hands.

"Governor Roosevelt," he said, "the others have greeted you with interest as a great American. I greet you with even more interest as the son of your father, the first Theodore Roosevelt."

"You knew my father?" Theodore asked.

"Indeed I did. I was an orphan, really just a waif selling newspapers on the streets of New York. Your father found me and sent me West, paying for my train ticket and for my early care with a Western family."

"And now you are Governor of Alaska."

"Yes, I gradually rose in the world," John Brady replied. "Thanks to your father, today I can greet his son as a fellow governor of a part of our great country."

How pleased his father would have been, thought Theodore. Some day he must tell the story of the newsboy who became a governor to the boys now living at the Newsboys' Lodging House.

Early in November, William McKinley and Theodore Roosevelt were elected, and the following March Edith took Alice and the younger children to see their father become Vice President of the United States. Ted, who was attending "prep" school at Groton, Massachusetts, was to meet her in Washington.

Unfortunately, Ted's train was late. When he arrived at the Senate Gallery, his mother and two aunts were already seated in the front row. The children were there, too, except three-year-old Quentin who had been left with a friend. Edith glanced at her oldest son in dismay. None of his clothes matched. His trousers were one color, his vest another, his coat still a third.

"Ted," she whispered, "I told you to wear your best clothes."

"I did," he protested. "These are my best trousers, my best vest, and my best coat, too."

Edith tried not to smile. Her eyes were on the door, through which her husband presently entered. How dignified he looked, as he made his inaugural speech. Later, in a cab on her way to have luncheon with Mrs. McKinley, she remembered how intently the audience had listened.

As the cab turned into a driveway, she saw the White House through a mist of rain. She had been here once before, as a sightseer, when she was fifteen. How thrilled she had been then, how thrilled she was now, as she thought of all the history that had been made beyond those tall white pillars. Abraham Lincoln had walked through the same front door.

After the inauguration, Theodore presided over the meetings of the Senate for five days. Then the members went home, not to meet again until December.

Until that time, his only official duty was to make the dedication speech at the Pan American Exposition which opened in May. This big fair in the city of Buffalo was held to celebrate the progress of the countries of North and South America, and the Vice President spoke of how much had been accomplished during the century just ended. A wilderness had been conquered and new nations established.

"We have made long strides in the right direction," he said, "but we have much yet to learn. The century upon which we have just entered must be one of tremendous triumph or one of tremendous failure for the whole human race, because more than ever before humanity is knit together in all its parts. . . . The prosperity of any one of us can best be attained by measures that will promote the prosperity of all."

Later that same summer of 1901, Theodore made two speaking tours that took him as far west as Minnesota, then East again. He was in Vermont on September 6th attending a reception at the home of a former governor of the state when he was called out of the room to take a telephone call. When he returned, his eyes were filled with tears.

"The President—" he began.

There was silence in the room. The guests drew closer. They knew that William McKinley had gone to Buffalo to attend the Pan American Exposition. The Vice President must have received some bad news.

"The President has been shot," he went on. "He was shot by some crazed anarchist. He is seriously wounded. I must go to him at once."

During the train ride to Buffalo Theodore hardly spoke. He was grieving for a friend. He also dreaded the thought that if William McKinley should die, he—Theodore Roosevelt—would be the President. He had hoped some day to be elected to that high office, but he did not want to come to it through the misfortune of another. He was much relieved, when he arrived at the house where the President was, to find that he was better. The doctors believed that he would soon be well.

Theodore's thoughts turned to Edith and the children, who were on a vacation in the Adirondacks. After a few days he joined them at a little cottage high in the mountains where they were staying. It had been raining when he arrived, but he never minded rain. He craved solitude, and the next morning he started on a long hike up Mount Marcy. With him went two guides and Corinne's two young sons. They ate their lunch beside a brook on a shelf of land, and when suddenly the mist cleared they looked out over one blue ridge rising beyond another in the distance.

"There wasn't a thought in my mind," Theodore said later, "but that the President would live. I was perfectly happy until I saw the runner coming."

The "runner," or messenger, worked at the Tahawus Club, which had the only telephone in that lonely region. He handed the Vice President a slip of paper. On it was written a message from a member of the Cabinet. Theodore's face was pale, as he turned to his companions.

"The President is worse. I must go back to the cottage."

It was dark by the time he reached it. The Tahawus Club was ten miles farther down the mountains, and Theodore sent the messenger to find out if any new message had come. Then he went to bed. He must get all the rest he could. He must be ready for whatever happened.

By eleven o'clock the messenger was back, knocking at the door. He carried several telegrams, which had been telephoned to the clubhouse. They were from William Loeb, Theodore's secretary. They said that the President was dying. A special train was waiting at North Creek, the nearest railroad station, to take the Vice President to Buffalo.

Outwardly calm, Theodore started to get ready. The messenger told him that arrangements had been made to drive him to North Creek. "But that is thirty-five or forty miles away," Edith protested. "The road is bad enough in daytime and in good weather. But after all this rain—"

She did not go on. She knew that her husband must leave, no matter how dangerous the journey.

In a few minutes a driver with a team and buckboard drew up before the cottage. Three times during the wild ride down the mountainside, the horses were changed and a new driver took over. A misty rain made the dark night seem even darker. Mike Cronin, the driver for the last sixteen-mile lap of the journey, could scarcely see the driving reins. But his horses knew the way. He had driven them many times over this same road, although never in such weather.

A lantern was fastened to the dashboard, and Mike glanced curiously at the passenger who sat beside him. Theodore held his watch in his hand, looking at it every few minutes in the flickering light. One of the horses stumbled.

"Mr. Roosevelt," said Mike, "there's a ticklish piece of road ahead of us. Maybe I'd better hold the team back."

"That doesn't matter. Push ahead!" Theodore replied.

For several minutes they raced over the rutted ground in silence. The next stretch of road had been cut into a steep hillside. "There's a dangerous curve ahead," Mike warned again. "If we upset we might pitch headlong down a hundred feet. It's a risky spot. Shall I slow down?"

"If you are not afraid, I am not," said Theodore. "Push ahead. How much farther do we have to go?"

He asked that same question again and again. In spite of the dangerous road, Mike made good time. His team covered the sixteen miles in one hour and forty-three minutes, and they reached North Creek in the first dim light of dawn. Theodore saw a train waiting on the track. His secretary, William Loeb, came toward him.

His voice was low. "Mr. President," he said.

William McKinley had died during the Vice President's ride through the dark night. Theodore Roosevelt, not yet forty-three years old, was now the President of the United States.

Theodore Roosevelt reached Buffalo that afternoon. In the home of a friend, in the presence of the Cabinet, he raised his right hand. "I do solemnly swear," he said, "that I will faithfully execute the office of President of the United States and will, to the best of my ability, preserve, protect, and defend the Constitution of the United States."

It was a quiet ceremony and all the more solemn for that reason. He had sent a message to his wife, and she started at once for Oyster Bay. After leaving the younger children there, she and Ted went on to Washington. She felt very sad because of what had happened to President McKinley. This time when she saw the White House it seemed a very gloomy place, but she knew that with the coming of six lively young Roosevelts, it would be a gay and happy home.

As soon as possible she returned to Sagamore Hill. She must close the house, and get the children ready for their journey to Washington. Edith was very proud of her husband, and her pride in him was shared by many—by his children, his sisters, and his friends. Joe Ferris out in Dakota and Bill Sewall up in Maine had decided a long time before that he had a good chance of becoming President. Now they were confident that the next time he would be *elected* to that high office. Mike Cronin never forgot the night when he became President the first time.

"I tell you, Mr. Roosevelt is a nervy man," he said. "I shall never drive over that dark road again without seeming to hear him say, 'Push along! Hurry up! Go faster!'"

In far-off Germany, Fräulein Anna, who was now Frau Fisher, remembered him as a boy of fourteen. She had told his mother then that she believed he might become President. "Perhaps as a result of my impulsive remark," she said to a magazine writer who went to interview her, "I have continually watched Theodore Roosevelt's career and have always been glad when he made a step forward in the world."

Edith had not yet returned when Theodore Roosevelt moved into the White House on September 22nd. He wanted some members of his own family to be with him on that first evening, so he had asked Bamie and Corinne and their husbands for dinner.

"Do you remember what day this is?" he asked them, as they sat at the table. "It is Father's birthday. I have realized it all day as I signed various papers."

An understanding smile flashed between him and Corinne. She knew how often their father had been in her brother's thoughts. He had tried to meet every problem as his father would have wished—with courage! How proud the first Theodore Roosevelt would have been, if he could have lived to see his small sickly son grow up to become the twenty-sixth President of the United States.

"I feel that it is a good omen that I begin my duties in this house on this day," said Theodore softly. "I feel as if my father's hand were on my shoulder, and as if there were a special blessing over the life that I am to live here."

Three years later Theodore Roosevelt was elected President in his own right. On Inauguration Day in 1905, he stood on the east portico of the Capitol before a vast multitude. Later, as he rode in the Inaugural Parade down Pennsylvania Avenue, he was cheered by thousands.

"How I wish," he wrote one of his cousins, "that Father could have lived to see that, too."

PRINTED IN U.S.A.